BEYOND THE FAIRWAYS TO FULFILMENT

Developing a success mindset for fulfilment both on and off the golf course.

CHRIS HYNES

Ark House Press
arkhousepress.com

© 2025 Chris Hynes | chrishynescoaching@outlook.com

All rights reserved. Apart from any fair dealing for the purpose of study, research, criticism, or review, as permitted under the Copyright Act, no part may be reproduced by any process without written permission.

Cataloguing in Publication Data:
Title: Beyond the Fairways to Fulfilment
ISBN: 978-1-7642308-6-5 (pbk)
Subjects: BIO016000   BIOGRAPHY & AUTOBIOGRAPHY / Sports; SEL021000   SELF-HELP / Motivational & Inspirational;

Design by initiateagency.com

Dedication

To Indigo and Jasmine, I dedicate this book to you. You always inspire me to be the best person and father I can be. You light up my life like a beautiful rainbow. I love you with all my heart, Daddy.

CONTENTS

Chapter 1 – Intention 1
Chapter 2 – Story 7
Chapter 3 – Faith 15
Chapter 4 – Inner Guide 23
Chapter 5 – Gratitude 31
Chapter 6 – Imagination 37
Chapter 7 – Visualisation 43
Chapter 8 – Accountability 51
Chapter 9 – Trust 57
Chapter 10 – Transition Space 65
Chapter 11 – The Now 73
Chapter 12 – Focus 81
Chapter 13 – Resilience 89
Chapter 14 – Six Core Needs 99
Chapter 15 – Peak State 107
Chapter 16 – Confidence 115
Chapter 17 – Self-Belief 123
Chapter 18 – Be-Do-Have 131

About the Author 141

ACKNOWLEDGEMENTS

I am deeply grateful to my mum and dad for their unwavering love and support, for instilling quality virtuous morals and values, and for the countless lifts to Werribee Park Golf Course that made my dreams possible. I love you both forever.

To my mentors and coaches – particularly Eric Lucas, Brett Lebroque and Jaemin Frazer – your guidance and encouragement shaped not only my career but also the person I am today.

I would like to express my heartfelt gratitude to my editor Dr Kerry Hansford for her exceptional skill and dedication in bringing my thoughts and concepts to life. Her meticulous editing has truly elevated my work, capturing my vision with precision and clarity. Thank you for your invaluable contribution and expertise.

My appreciation to Jay Hynes Photography for his skill, visual talent and incredible imagination in capturing the perfect cover shot.

My thanks to my equipment suppliers: Mizuno for quality clubs, Kari Lajosi for great putters, in combination with Titleist balls and Footjoy clothing.

As you read through this book, you may or may not be familiar with the Sanctuary Lakes Golf Course, a Greg Norman/Bob Harrison design, which opened in 1999. Through the developer's great vision, the land was transformed from a former salt plain into a championship links-style golf course, featuring Santa Anna Couch fairways, hardy fescues and native grasses, and Greg Norman's signature bunkers.

And to every golfer, athlete, leader, and individual who has inspired me to explore this journey of personal and professional growth, this book says thank you.

INTRODUCTION

What if the only thing standing between you and your best life – on the golf course and beyond – is your mindset?

It's not your swing, your equipment, or even your practice regimen. It's the beliefs you hold, the stories you tell yourself, and the way you handle challenges. If you're reading this book, it's because you already sense that there's untapped potential within you – potential to play better golf, and more importantly, to live a more fulfilling life.

You desire to see the seeds in your heart bear fruit in your life. Golf is more than just a sport; it's a mirror reflecting the lessons and challenges we face in life. It's an arena where your mindset determines your success as much, if not more, than your physical skill.

This book is your guide to mastering that mindset – because when you change the way you think, you change the way you play, and you transform the way you live.

To play golf to your full potential, you will need to confront and overcome your insecurities and limiting beliefs. You must take responsibility for your thoughts, actions and outcomes, both on and off the course. One of my biggest breakthroughs came when I had a transformational epiphany: No one's opinion really matters to me or can impact on me; the only opinion that truly matters is my own opinion of myself. This realisation was liberating. It allowed me to break free from the chains of doubt and the need for external validation, which had been holding me back from reaching my full potential.

In this journey, you will discover your true identity, not the false identity shaped by the expectations of others. You will learn to live your best life from a place of being, not merely doing. This process involves forging your unique blueprint for success, recognising that there is only one you. Striving to be a clone of someone else would be a disservice to yourself, as a golfer and as a person.

The pursuit of your best golf will lead you into deep, dark caves, but with courage and faith, you will emerge triumphant. True success is not defined by riches but by the bravery to live the life you were born to live. Often, the lessons learned on the golf course will reveal your life's destiny.

Golf, like life, is the pursuit of mastery, not the illusion of perfection. It requires you to follow fundamentals and principles, to be patient and resilient. Both golf and life will take you to places where you will be tempted to give up. The loud, hollow voice of doubt will scream lies, hoping you will forfeit your destiny through deception and succumb by quitting.

But your resilience will support you. Your ability to accept that change and sacrifice are necessary, along with your adaptability, self-discipline and focus, will rebalance you. Your ability to live and play golf in your optimal state will give you access to self-discovery, revealing a highly resourceful person who has the focus and strategic capacity to overcome challenges. Through faith, courage and authentic living, you will display a mastery that leads to a fulfilling life.

I know this because it's been my journey. For years, I longed to live up to my potential both on and off the golf course. It wasn't until I worked with a life coach and willingly faced my insecurities and limiting beliefs that I broke free from the chains of misunderstanding and started living free of doubt and insecurities, enjoying the freedom of being authentic – fearless of condemnation and fully expressing my best self.

INTRODUCTION

There Are Principles, Laws, and Fundamentals that Lead to Predictable Outcomes

If you plant apple seeds, you will reap apple trees. If you think quality thoughts and take congruent action, you will live a quality life. Many laws and principles govern our lives, often subconsciously. This book will increase your awareness of these laws and principles, equipping you to harness them for a fruitful and fulfilling existence.

Personal Transformation and Peak Performance

Two significant events led to the creation of this book. First, my own personal transformation, which renewed my love for golf and rekindled other important aspects of my life. Second, a peak performance experience during a table tennis match. This experience was nothing short of spiritual a moment of flow where time seemed to stand still – I was fully present, fully engaged, and performing at my best. This experience, which stemmed from a conversation with a mentor, led to a deeper understanding of the requirements for peak performance:

i. Intention

Be clear about the outcome you desire. Your intention is the energy that sets the course for your actions and decisions. It is the guiding force that aligns your efforts toward achieving the success you envision.

ii. Trust

Trust in your skills, preparation, and most importantly, yourself. This trust is the foundation upon which confidence is built, allowing you to perform at your best without hesitation or doubt.

iii. Wanting or Needing

Let go of the need for success to validate your worth as a person. Instead, focus on the process, knowing that your value is intrinsic and not dependent on outcomes. This detachment from results allows for a more relaxed and optimal performance.

iv. Presence

Fully engage in the moment with awareness of your surroundings and inner experience, free of judgement and attachment. Presence allows you to react with precision and clarity, making the most of every situation.

v. Resilience

Respond to setbacks and challenges with inner strength and determination that are congruent with the level of success you desire. Resilience is about maintaining your composure and focus, turning obstacles into opportunities for growth and improvement.

vi. The Right Avatar

Be the best authentic you, expressing the very best of yourself – your skillset, your mindset, and your toolset. This is the vehicle that will enable you to achieve the success you want. The way you dress, the language you use, and the demeanour you present are all part of embodying the successful version of yourself.

Before the Magic

Often, before a peak performance, you recall the moments leading up to it – the preparation, the mindset, the subtle shifts in perspective. The same was true for

INTRODUCTION

my friend Steve and me before what would become his lowest round of golf to date.

We spent time in the locker room, using myofascial release techniques to loosen tight muscles. We hydrated, grabbed a smoothie, and discussed the parallels between my peak performance in table tennis and its application to golf. As we warmed up, everything felt smooth; our bodies ready. We headed to the short game area to hit a few chip shots, focusing on feel and precision, while getting a sense of the green speed. Then, we moved to the range to take a few full swings, dialling in our tempo and ball striking. After that, we spent some time on longer putts, gradually honing our touch. We finished by holing a few 3-footers as confidence builders before making our way to the first tee. With our routines complete, we felt fully prepared, both mentally and physically, as we stepped up to start the round.

The Sage

As we waited on the first tee, my thoughts drifted to a dream state, imagining an ancient sage. In my mind's eye, the sage took form in the course itself – every fairway, every green and every hazard reflecting its wisdom. The sage, an ancient figure reminiscent of King Solomon, radiated wisdom and understanding, drawing people from all walks of life who sought his guidance, especially in matters of life and golf. He was not just a figure of knowledge, but a mentor whose insights helped others unlock their fullest potential. The course was no longer an obstacle to be feared, but a challenge to be embraced, a strategy to be mastered. Each course challenge was an opportunity to show my true ability by demonstrating faith in myself, overcoming doubt. Meeting these challenges would reward me with the gifts of improvement, confidence, and growth.

Standing on the first tee felt like stepping into a mystical journey – a journey where every moment would bring me closer to my true self. The course was not merely a test of skill but a reflection of my mindset and beliefs, bringing awareness to those thoughts and beliefs that were either helping or hindering me, guiding me to refine and upgrade them as needed.

This mindset shift was profound. It wasn't about conquering the course; it was about partnering with it, allowing it to guide me towards my best performance. As I shared this story with Steve, we both began to see the course and our game through a new lens.

Your Journey Begins

As you journey through the chapters ahead, take the time to understand each principle, apply it to your life, and watch as both your game and your life are transformed. This is your invitation to step into a world where mastery is not just possible, but inevitable – if you are willing to commit to the process.

CHAPTER 1
INTENTION

"Intention is the energy that transforms the unseen into the physical."

Hole 1

Our intention in life is like the spark that ignites a fire. It sets in motion actions that produce outcomes. Therefore, in life and golf, it's imperative to be hyper-intentional about the outcomes we desire. As a coach in various fields, particularly in golf, I often ask people about their intentions. Many respond, "I will try to…." To this, I reply that the word "try" insinuates little, if any, intent. Therefore, it is not conducive to achieving a desired outcome. Intention is like the first domino that gets knocked over, setting in motion the consequences of an action. Our golf score is simply a by-product of an intention followed by various interconnected moments and events that followed that initial intention.

I am always intentional about my optimal state and mindset before I play golf. I am hyper-intentional about being in my best state and maintaining that throughout the entire round. I am intentional about my pre-game warm-up, my golfing strategy, and maintaining my energy through good nutrition and physical fitness. Now, I'm ready to play.

Steve and I stood on the familiar first tee of a 379 metre par 4 feeling a profound connection to the course. The fairway appeared more luminous than ever, and the bunkers and rough blurred into nothingness. I felt a quiet stillness within, and the usual chatter in my mind was silent.

I teed up the ball with balance and ease, pressing it into the tee. I stood behind the ball with clear intentions for the shot. From these intentions came visualisation, and from visualisation came feel. I took a calming nasal breath, walked into the ball, focused on the shot's starting line and shape, and felt the shot. I aimed my club, took a glance down the starting line, and aligned my body to the club. With another glance at the target, a brief look back at the ball, and void of conscious thought, I made a swing. The ball collided with the middle of the club face, feeling perfect through the grip and into my hands. It flew straight at the target, resting near the crest of a hill.

Steve went through his routine, which had improved significantly over the past few months. He used to play golf in conflict, wrestling with technical deficiencies like casting and flipping. These issues were personal to him, but after mindset work, he now stood on the first tee with a far better attitude, looking more at ease and ready to enjoy his golf. Steve's best shots have a nice draw. He aimed just right of centre, settled over the ball, took his two customary looks, and hit a beautiful soft draw that finished in the middle of the fairway.

I am consistently clear about my intentions when playing golf. My intentions vary depending on the situation. In a competitive round, I am intentional about every shot, having a great strategy, maintaining a positive emotional state, being 100% committed to each shot, and enjoying the round. When playing with friends who seek help with their game, my focus shifts to serving them best, but I remain intentional about enjoying myself and achieving desired outcomes.

We reached Steve's ball, which was 142 metres from the hole. He decided on a three-quarter 7-iron, aiming for a right-to-left draw. He took a couple of practice swings, then set up, took his waggles, looked, and hit a crisp 7-iron. It finished safely on the green, slightly long, and right of the hole.

INTENTION

As I approached my ball, a gentle breeze blew slightly off the right and against me. I had 128 metres to the pin, which was slightly left of centre on the green. The breeze seemed to whisper the shot into my ear – start the ball at the centre of the green and let the breeze work it slightly back to the hole. I agreed wholeheartedly and went through my routine, feeling the shot draw soft on the breeze. The first creation is the thought – now to manifest it. A calming breath set my routine in motion. I aimed at the centre of the green, aligned my club face and body, took one last look at the starting line, and I made a smooth swing with a 9-iron. The ball flew perfectly, bouncing twice and gripping the green hard, resting three feet below the hole.

We marked and cleaned our balls. Steve walked the length of his putt to see and feel the line. Often, the practice putting green speed can differ from the on-course greens, so it's important to compare the feel under your feet, especially on the first hole.

I marked my ball with my 1956 Australian penny, a sentimental family coin. Cleaning my ball with a fresh towel is always part of my putting routine, as even a grass stain or small piece of dirt or mud can cause a missed putt. Steve had a 30-foot birdie putt. We had recently practiced putting drills together, focusing on lag putting. The goal was to leave at least two out of three putts within one foot short of the hole. Steve walked his line, assessed his putt, and was intentional about lagging his long putts. If it goes in, great – if not, he has a tap-in. He hit a nice putt that finished inches from the hole, tapping in for par.

I had a 3-foot birdie putt. Before leaving the practice putting green, I had drilled several 3-foot putts, making them all. Trusting my routine and execution, I replaced my ball, pocketed my penny, and set my intentions on the pace and line of the putt – inside the right edge of the hole. After a couple of rhythmic practice strokes, I aimed my eyes, then my putter, then my stance, then looked at the intended line and fired. The ball came off the sweet spot, and I knew it was in before it reached the hole. A solid birdie 3 to start the round.

Sage Advice on Intention

- Your intentions give clarity to your desired outcome.
- Your intentions captivate your attention. Your attention guides the flow of your energy.
- The clearer your intentions, the stronger your commitment.

Intention

Intention comes at a price. It will cost you your two most precious resources, your time and your energy. Therefore, invest these two precious resources wisely with the intention that the outcome is purposeful and fulfilling.

A fulfilling life begins with living an intentional life. Once you decide (from the Latin *decidere*, meaning 'to cut off') to live intentionally, you must be deliberate about the language you use and the words you speak. Be intentional about your thoughts and take captive any negative ones. Your intentions are the first step toward your desired outcome. Intention acts as a compass, guiding your focus. Where attention goes, energy flows. The more energy directed toward your intention, the stronger your commitment and resilience becomes.

Your intentions run parallel to your beliefs. Faith – a belief in the outcome you desire – acts as a supportive structure that keeps the energy of your intentions high. Conversely, if your attention shifts towards doubt, you become distracted, and your intentions dissipate.

Disruption often follows intention. Use disruption to contrast and refine your intentions. In golf, this occurs when you set intentions for a shot, visualise a positive outcome, but are faced with a bunker or hazard. Recognise this as a natural occurrence and refocus with greater clarity and commitment, using this interference to your advantage. Believe that all things happen for your benefit.

To maintain the integrity of your intentions, be clear about the outcome you desire and why you desire it. Set up an environment that supports maintaining your intentions. Tour players have caddies who really help and support their intentions through positive encouragement. For a player without a caddy, their own self-talk can play this role, through positive and encouraging self-talk. Establish daily habits that align with your intentions, such as just ten minutes a day of practice swings on an aspect of your game or ten minutes of functional exercise. Build a support team of family and friends, keep a mental picture of the desired outcome, and be energised by how you will feel upon achieving it.

Intentions are birthed by imagination and words. Every word is like a seed, and every seed is like a deed, and every deed will reap a consequence. Form a mental image of the desired outcome and bring it to life with words. Those words set intentions in motion. For example, with a 30 metre pitch shot, imagine the ball going in, then use words like 'hole it' or 'in it goes' to fuel your intention. Your subconscious will work to bring this intention and belief to fruition.

In a round of golf, you will have multiple intentions. The obvious one is to play well but being more specific helps. Maintain an optimal performance state, have a sound strategy, keep a consistent routine, hit the ball out of the middle of the club, and accept below-standard shots or unforeseen circumstances. Be your authentic self.

Being clear about your intentions and staying committed to them gives you the best chance of achieving the results you desire. Hyper-intentionality about what you say and the language you use is the starting point to living an intentional and fruitful life.

Sage Questions on Intention

1. Being intentional with the words you speak is imperative to success in life. How could you be more intentional about the words you speak and maintain a high standard in doing so?

_____
_____
_____
_____

2. Are your day-to-day intentions aligned with your purpose in life? How could you better align these two important aspects?

_____
_____
_____
_____

3. When setting your intentions for a desired outcome, how do you manage to stay detached from the outcome and focus on the process?

_____
_____
_____
_____

A Model of Intention: Moe Norman

Moe Norman, a famous Canadian golfer, epitomised intention. He was extremely intentional about many aspects of his life, but none more so than his golf game. He was super intentional about refining his unique swing, despite ridicule. There are legendary stories of Moe hitting over a thousand balls a day, highly intentional about each shot. He often liked to say, "There are only good shots in my bag; I only see good shots." Moe's incredible results stemmed from his intentional focus, positive inner dialogue, and unwavering commitment. He visualised perfect shots, repeated them in his mind, and then executed them with precision. Moe's story teaches us the power of unwavering intention and belief in achieving extraordinary results.

CHAPTER 2
STORY

"Whether you're aware of it or not, your life is just a story. You are the director of your story. It is your responsibility to make it a story worthy of the time and effort you have put into it."

Hole 2

Walking to the second tee, Steve grinning, said, "So what do you think this ancient sage would look like?"

I smiled and said, "He would have to be a small, oriental-type gentleman with kind eyes but a look on his face that displayed great wisdom."

"Do you think he would have been a golfer?" Steve asked.

"I think he would have been good at everything he tried. Whether it was fishing, table tennis, or golf, and for the time he played, he would have had a brilliant short game. A chess master. A great meditator of truth. He would be calm, wise, and a great caddy and mentor."

"All that you think," said Steve.

"All that and a fair bit more, I imagine. He would be the calm in any storm, and if you looked into his eyes, you would see a loving soul that brought a smile to your face."

Steve said, "Kind of like the grandfather everyone would want."

"For sure," I replied.

The second hole was a 155 metre par 3. It was slightly downhill and slightly downwind. I spoke words that created a story. As I stood on the tee looking at the hole, I said, "I am going to hit an 8-iron. It won't move much directionally due to it being downwind. I will hit it high, so it lands soft and stops quickly." The words I was speaking were creating images and a story in my head. I then let the story become a visualised picture, which then became a feeling in my body, that then became my preparation for that shot. My practice swing felt effortless and automatic. I approached the ball with my consistent routine, took a last look at my starting line just two metres right of the hole, then a very brief look back at the ball, and set my swing in motion. The ball flew off the sweet spot, it felt light off the club, and sailed on my intended line. There was a combination of thoughts while watching it fly at my intended target – thoughts of, "wow, that was effortless," and slight surprise that this was travelling just as I had felt it would. It landed about four metres short of the pin, took a bounce, and then settled a metre past the pin. Steve hit a solid 7-iron to about 24 feet long, right of the hole. Quite similar to his position on the first green.

As we walked off the tee, Steve asked, "So, if you could ask the sage one question, what would it be?"

I said, "I would ask him how do I access the best of me? The best of me that could birdie every hole. We have played this course quite a bit – I have birdied every hole and eagled all but one of the par fives. All those birdies and eagles, all the great shots and great putts are stored in my subconscious. It's like I put them in a safety deposit box; it would be great to take them out anytime I like and use them as often as I choose. I know I'm going to hit shots even better in the future, but all my past great shots are more than enough to produce course record scores. That's what I would like to access. What would you ask the sage?"

"Well, now you have put it that way, I guess all my best-ever shots would accumulate into sub-par rounds every time, and I would be more than happy to sign off on that for the rest of my golfing life…" We both pondered that as we approached the green.

Peak performances in golf are void of conscious thought – they are indeed the result of playing through our subconscious, the vault of our greatest shots. A golfer standing over the ball with swing thoughts is a golfer strangling the flow of a peak performance. You hear of golfers describing playing with a swing thought or two, but certainly never more than that. This goes back to trust in peak performance. You trust you have done the work. You trust your swing. You don't need your conscious mind disrupting the flow. People with more than one or two thoughts are not going to be interviewed for playing well. Tiger was often asked what he was thinking over the ball – his response was, "I wasn't." He would say, "I don't remember anything over the ball, just seeing it fly off."

Steve's lag putting drills were certainly paying dividends as he rolled his birdie putt to within inches again for another tap-in par. You always want to leave tap-ins from long range. The best players in the world make less than ten percent of putts from 25 feet; the focus should be on having a stress-free two-putt. There's an old saying: "Pros that have long putts for par and dogs that chase cars don't last long."

I went through my usual process of marking and cleaning my ball. I took a quick look at the putt; no need to complicate it, it's straight, slightly downhill, and only needs to be stroked as though it's a 2 foot putt. I calmly stroked it into the centre of the cup.

Sage Advice on Story

- Your life is a story.
- It's your responsibility.
- Every disempowering story is a fuelled by a lie.

Story

Life is often described metaphorically as a movie. On their deathbeds, people often see their lives flash before their eyes like a movie in fast-forward. This is a fitting description of life, which is made up of a continuum of moments that culminate in events and experiences. These moments and events come together to form what we call life.

Initially, these moments and events are void of meaning until you give them meaning. You attach meaning or judgement to an event or experience to make sense of it. Humans are inherently curious beings who like to give things meaning to understand them.

The most disempowering stories that lead to limiting or restrictive beliefs are often created between the ages of 0 to 7, and they are inevitably a misunderstanding that becomes a lie. A combination of what you made up and what your parents, grandparents and community told you to believe form most of your current beliefs. The problem is many of these beliefs hold you back from living the life or story you truly want to live.

That fitter, healthier, stronger person you want to be. That much better and more confident golfer you want to be. That true and better version of yourself that's screaming inside to come out is held back by childhood limiting beliefs that are not even true. One of the challenges in changing your story and updating it is that you're often unaware that the story you're living is the very thing holding you back.

When you become aware that these limiting beliefs are the obstacles holding you back, you come to understand that beliefs have a structure, a framework. Therefore, they can be deconstructed and reconstructed. The way to deconstruct a belief is through doubt.

Doubt, you might think. Yes, doubt. Say you hold the belief that you are not a good putter.

- OK ask, have I ever one-putted or have I ever holed some 10 – 20 foot putts? The answer is likely Yes.
- OK, so at times I have holed some nice putts, which would be classified as good putting. Again, the answer is Yes.
- OK, so you do have the capacity to putt well at times. The answer, of course, is Yes.
- So, it's not true that you always putt poorly. The answer is, well, I suppose not.

With this doubt, the story can be pulled apart and rebuilt. Once you rebuild the new belief that you can putt well, your subconscious will do all it can to support this new belief. This will prompt you to improve your technique, to get a putting lesson, to get fitted properly for a putter – all actions resulting from a new belief.

Sometimes experiences outside of golf impact your thoughts and beliefs in a way that adversely affects your golf. Whatever the case, the process is the same. To deconstruct and reconstruct, you must go back to where the belief began, but with a skilled mindset coach, this is a simple process.

First, answer the question: "What do I want?" Be aware that your limiting beliefs could also be holding you back. From there, have a strong desire and commitment to take the necessary action to get what you want. It is possible, I can assure you of that.

Once you have dismantled the old belief, you must replace it and rebuild a new and empowering belief. The old space that held the limiting belief should be filled with a new empowering one. If you don't fill that space, another limiting belief would take its place. There is a far greater bias towards holding negative beliefs; they queue up to find a home. So, as soon as you have cleared one out, replace it with a strong, positive and empowering belief.

Our stories start with the words we speak both internally and externally. They start in our heads, connect to our hearts, set off emotions and physical feelings, and go to our hands as empowering or disempowering actions. So be impeccable with your words. Speak only positive, empowering words. Your words are seeds that will grow into the fruits of your life.

As you journey through life and golf, it's crucial to view both as paths to mastery rather than destinations defined by outcomes and scores. Embrace the process and find joy in the pursuit of improvement and the lessons learned along the way. Mastery is a lifelong endeavour, filled with ups and downs, but the true satisfaction comes from your dedication to the craft and your love of the game. When you focus on mastery, you detach from the pressure of the scorecard and immerse yourself in the experience, finding fulfilment in each swing, each round, and each moment on the course.

Remember, you are the director, narrator and star actor in your story. Make it one that, when your time is up in this world and it flashes before your eyes, brings a smile to your face and joy to your heart. Be bold, be courageous, live out a great story.

Sage Questions on Story

1. Reflecting on the stories you find yourself replaying the most in your mind, how can you reframe these stories so that they empower you and align with your purpose and goals?

   _____
   _____
   _____
   _____

2. How can you change a current belief story about your golf game that is limiting your ability to a more empowering and motivating story that will raise your performance and enjoyment on the course?

_____
_____
_____
_____

3. What is a current story that you could upgrade that would enable you to enjoy your golf all the time, irrespective of your score?

_____
_____
_____
_____

A Model of Story: Lee Trevino

One of the greatest storytellers and legends in golf is the Mexican American professional Lee Trevino. He grew up in poverty in a small shack in Texas, teaching himself to play golf with makeshift clubs and balls. From a young age, Trevino told himself a story: he was going to rise from the ashes of poverty and become one of the greatest golfers of all time. He visualised, dreamed, and practised with unwavering self-belief, always maintaining a positive and upbeat attitude.

Despite facing numerous challenges, including being struck by lightning during a tournament, Trevino lived out his incredible story. He went on to win six major championships, including two US Opens, two Open Championships, and two PGA Championships. In total, he won 29 PGA Tour events worldwide. From a young age, the stories he constantly ran in his mind manifested his success in the physical world.

Trevino's ability to live out his empowering story was fuelled by his intentions, resilience and self-belief. He is a man who courageously embodied the power of a positive and purposeful narrative. Let his story remind you that the set of sentences you play in your mind can indeed shape your reality.

Your life is a story that you write with every thought, word, and action. Embrace the power of intention and belief, and you can create a narrative that leads to the success and fulfilment you desire. Just like Lee Trevino, let the stories you tell yourself be ones of triumph, resilience and unwavering self-belief, leading to a fulfilling life.

CHAPTER 3
FAITH

"Faith, the belief in the outcome you desire."

Hole 3

As we walked to the third tee, Steve shared how much faith he had in his practice and achieving his goals. His confidence, especially in his lag putting, was at an all-time high thanks to the drills he had been practicing. This confidence stemmed from putting in the work, building trust in his abilities, and believing that all his practice would produce his desired outcomes. This significantly boosted his faith.

When you have faith in what you are doing or desiring to do, it creates a powerful motivation and resilience to focus on the long term, especially in challenging times. When you have absolute faith in life or golf, it allows you to immerse yourself in the mastery of the process. Like a potter, you have faith that you can produce the object you desire. You have faith that all the hard work will be worth it. You know that challenges and setbacks are part of the process, and you don't get overwhelmed by them.

The third hole, a 342m par 4, runs in the same direction as the 2nd hole, so it was a little down breeze, slightly right to left. The hole also runs right to left. I could see the pin was cut left, so it was best to be right of centre, the hole swept right to the left almost like a long hit driver that draws late. As I stood on the tee and looked down the fairway, there were several mower strips that really stood out in colour. I smiled as though the ancient sage had highlighted these strips of fairway as the path to take. I visualised following that path with a soft drawing driver. I teed up my ball on the left side of the tee and hit a nice flighted drive, just as I had visualised, which finished in the mayor's office, right of centre.

The contrast when you are in the flow with golf and when you are struggling with it is like night and day. When you're in the flow, it's simple – the mind is quiet, you choose a shot, feel it and with complete trust you simply set up and swing with supreme faith and confidence. When you're struggling, there's always a battle with excessive swing thoughts, too much head chatter, wrestling for swing feels, and too much time trying to think your way to playing well, which won't happen.

Steve had a couple of practice swings and said, "You know what, my body feels so supple that my swing feels like it did in my 30s," which was some 20 years ago for him.

With that, he teed his ball precisely where I had, on the left side of the tee, and hit a drive that finished just left of centre.

Steve had 92 metres to a tight left pin. From his angle, the very big and deep left green side bunker was a reminder to aim right of the hole. It was a knockdown wedge for Steve, and his intended target was a good 15 feet right of the pin and ideally a couple of metres short. This left an uphill putt. He made a compact swing, and the ball jumped off a little hot. "Wow," he cried, "I felt like I hardly hit that. My pivot felt so free; I think it was giving me a bit more power!" His ball sailed past the pin and came to rest about 30 feet long and right. "Sure looked like a solid swing," I said.

Steve and I had recently been doing scoring zone drills together. Using our on-course routine, we did a 3-ball drill from 30, 70 and 100 metres where, we each hit shots, combined the total distance where our balls finished from the hole, and divided by 3. To measure this, we stepped out the distance as 1 full step = 3 feet, 2 full steps = 6 feet and 3 full steps = 9 feet. Say from 30 metres my first ball finished 6 feet away, my second ball was 3 feet away, and my third shot was 3 feet away, a total of 12 feet for 3 shots. On average, I was 4 feet away for the 3 shots.

I did this three times each day. There were periods where I progressively got better, and that was fun and exciting. Then one day, from 30 metres, I holed one of the shots and hit my next two shots to one foot each. My new standard became under one foot, and when I practised, I strived to meet this goal. And when I played, my intention and belief was that from 30 metres, I was likely to hit it to one foot; however, I was never attached to the outcome or had expectations. Again, this is a great example of how the peak performance code plays out. You trust because you did the work.

There is no wanting or needing anything from the shot to validate your worth. You know your value and worth as a human is not attached to this shot, and you know you have a great short game and don't need to prove it. You're playing the right game, you're a great short game artist, and you act like that person – you have the right avatar, which includes a great attitude, you dress like a good player, and you have wedges that are clean and in good condition.

It was a little more than a 9 o'clock backswing on the Dave Pelz wedge swing system with my 58-degree wedge.

Dave Pelz became a short game guru in the early 1980s. His pitching system works around a clock face of 7:30, 9.00 and 10:30 length swing. So, a third of a backswing for 7:30, half backswing for 9.00, and a three-quarter backswing for 10:30. The time and swing length references are in relation to the left arm for right-handed golfers, imagining 12.00 o'clock at your head, 6.00 o'clock at your feet, 9.00 o'clock at your right hip, and 3.00 o'clock the follow-through side at your left hip. Players do this for three or four wedges, effectively giving nine to 12 different distances. Some distances overlap, but it is basically a system whereby your swing length determines your shot length.

As I was waiting for Steve to play his shot, a beautiful small rainbow appeared from behind the hole, acting as a trajectory for the shot I was about to hit. I picked a spot in the rainbow that was the peak of my intended ball flight. I couldn't help but think that this ancient sage had a little more influence beyond the parameters of this course. With the absolute surety, I went through my routine of matching a practice swing to the intended shot. I took a deep breath to control my excitement and confidence. Although I had visualised a very good shot, I wanted to be present. I walked in, took my setup, and looked at the spot in the rainbow. I looked back at the ball and made a compact pivot-driven swing. The contact was strong and sweet, and the ball climbed gently up the rainbow. You could sense the spin on the ball as it landed about pin high, bounced six feet past, and came spinning back, missing the hole by inches as it settled less than two feet below the hole.

I smiled at the rainbow, took a moment to soak in its beauty and expressed my gratitude to it through my intentions. We marked and cleaned our balls. Steve walked down the line of his putt to get a feel for the green. It was a similar type of putt to his first. He went through his routine and kept his head down until the putt was a fair way down its path. He stared intently. "Be good," he said, as though the golf ball would actually listen. He kept looking intently and started to walk to his right as though he was looking for a better angle to watch it. "Do it," he said, and in it went. "Yes, what a putt," he said, excited by the early birdie.

I smiled and said, "Well done mate, great putt." I replaced my ball, took one last look. No practice swing as I don't need to get the feel of a short putt – I have hit a lot of them – and tapped it in for my third straight birdie.

We walked to the next tee, and I shared with Steve how I used the rainbow to help flight my previous approach. I hinted that I thought it was there to help me with my shot, and just as we were both admiring its splendour, it disappeared back into the atmosphere.

Sage Advice on Faith

- Faith is a transformational superpower.
- Faith never guarantees an outcome, but it gives you a much better chance than doubt.
- Faith requires a growth mindset; and as such, ensures the results will bring about new learnings and growth potential.

Faith

The root word of faith is the Latin word *fides*, meaning 'to trust.' This is the same root for the word 'confidence.' Thus, faith, confidence and trust are intrinsically linked, supporting each other in a symbiotic relationship. Faith is not just a spiritual concept but a practical one that manifests itself in our everyday lives, including on the golf course.

People exhibit faith in their daily routines without even realising it. You book your next game of golf with faith that you'll be alive to play it. You get into your car with faith that it will start and get you to the course. You tee up your first drive with faith that your driver's head won't fly off. This kind of faith is often automatic, but it becomes crucially tested in high-pressure situations, such as needing a good drive on the last hole to win a match or holing a 3 foot putt for victory.

The challenge with doubt is that it can infiltrate your mind at the most critical moments. It has the advantage of certainty, one of the six core human needs. Doubt gathers past evidence to support its claims, reminding you of the times you've missed that crucial putt. This certainty makes doubt feel powerful and convincing.

The battle between faith and doubt is acute, because faith operates on trust and future projections without the concrete evidence that doubt can muster. Imagine a bucket of clear water representing faith. A single cup of black dye, symbolising doubt, can taint the entire bucket. Conversely, pouring a cup of clear water into a bucket of black-dyed water (doubt) has little impact. This analogy illustrates why doubt can feel inherently stronger than faith.

However, doubt is just a belief in an undesirable outcome. It relies on a story to stay alive. By deconstructing the story behind doubt, you can weaken its hold. For example, doubt may tell you that you've missed a one metre putt before. Counter this by reminding yourself that you've holed hundreds of similar putts. Present evidence of your success to destabilise doubt.

Belief is like a coin with two sides: faith and doubt. Faith is the belief in the outcome you desire, while doubt is the belief in the outcome you don't want. Both are beliefs and logically, choosing a belief that serves you is the best course of action. However, understanding why people choose doubt can be enlightening.

According to Tony Robbins (American author, coach and speaker), humans have six core needs: certainty, variety, significance, love and connection, growth, and contribution. Doubt meets the need for certainty by relying on past experiences. Faith, on the other hand, lacks this certainty and operates without evidence, making it harder for some to embrace.

Ultimately, faith is a choice over doubt. Like a muscle, the more you choose and use faith, the stronger it becomes in your life. Faith is the rocket fuel for motivation, the sledgehammer to the wall of setbacks and challenges, the calming influence for anxiety, and the foundation of resilience. It is a superpower that can transform your golfing experience; and indeed, your life.

Faith is a vital component of a successful person's mindset. It empowers you to face challenges with confidence, to persist through setbacks, and to envision and achieve your goals. By cultivating a deep belief in your abilities and the process, you set the stage for remarkable performances and transformative growth in your golfing journey. Embrace faith as your guiding light and watch as it illuminates the path to your fullest potential.

FAITH

Sage Questions on Faith

1. Reflect on a time when you had unwavering faith in achieving a specific goal, whether in golf or another area of your life. What steps did you take to maintain that faith, and how did it influence your actions and mindset throughout the process?

   _____
   _____
   _____
   _____

2. How do you handle moments of doubt and uncertainty on the course or in life? Do you have processes that help you realign with your faith in achieving your goals during these challenging times?

   _____
   _____
   _____
   _____

3. Faith requires a source to exist. What is your source of faith and is it sustainable?

   _____
   _____
   _____
   _____

A Model of Faith: Bernhard Langer and Scottie Scheffler

Bernhard Langer's journey in professional golf is a testament to the power of faith. Known for his incredible resilience and unwavering belief in his abilities,

Langer's career is filled with moments that highlight the role of faith in achieving greatness.

He holds the European Tour record for most consecutive cuts made – 72 in a row between 1980 and 1984 – and the most wins on the PGA Tour Champions with 46 titles as of 2024, including multiple senior majors. In 2023, at the age of 65, Langer became the oldest player ever to win a senior major. Remarkably, many of these victories came while battling the putting yips – a condition that often crumbles the strongest of competitors. Yet, with the faith of a mustard seed, Langer overcame these trials, proving that true belief can move even the most immovable mountains.

Similarly, Scottie Scheffler has emerged as one of the most successful sporting stars on the planet today, and he, too, leads with faith. Scheffler makes no secret of the order in his life: God first, then family, then golf. His calm demeanour, grounded in unwavering faith, is reflected in an extraordinary statistic – he has won all 10 tournaments in which he has held the 54-hole lead. On the morning of what would become his first major victory at the U.S. Masters, Scheffler admitted he was overcome with emotion and doubt, curled up in tears until his wife Meredith reminded him of who he is and where his strength comes from. That day, he played with great courage and faith securing the Green Jacket and setting the tone for a career defined by faith under pressure.

Both Langer and Scheffler demonstrate that faith is more than belief in self – it is trust in something greater, confidence in preparation, and peace in the process. It is the invisible anchor that enables calmness under any circumstances. Their victories display skill and commitment and are living examples of what happens when faith becomes the foundation.

Let their stories encourage you to build your life and your game on something deeper. Faith calms your mind, regulates your emotions and allows your hands to execute your skills truly. When pressure rises and doubt whispers, remember the source of true strength and keep your eyes fixed on that.

CHAPTER 4
INNER GUIDE

"Listen to that wise inner voice. Take the first step; nothing more, nothing less; and watch the magic of life unfold."

Hole 4

The fourth hole was a 500 metre par five. It's easy to get ahead of yourself on a reachable par 5 and pencil in a birdie when you are still on the tee. It requires that you be very intentional and focused on the shot at hand. The breeze was just slightly off the right and slightly into our faces. A big dam on the left and a bunker in the middle of the fairway meant that the fairway was effectively half its usual distance wide in that area. The right of the bunker made it a definite three-shot hole. I used a chimney in the far distance as my line down the left side of the fairway, between the dam and the bunker. It suited my eye well.

Sometimes a hole just simply doesn't suit your eye, and when that's the case, you are best served playing a shot that you are comfortable and confident in playing. That's when you listen to your inner guide to help you feel the shot that will work. I was mindful of the potential dangers that the hole presented, but I was now focused on my target – the chimney – and a nice 21/7 tempo swing that produced my best quality shots. I went through my routine with the intention of swinging with my optimal tempo; however, I also intended to hit with aggression to get it a little further down the fairway. It's fine to swing it aggressively, providing it matches your tempo. There's a difference between swinging aggressively with tempo and swinging it fast with no tempo. I took aim at the chimney, made a great pivot back and through, the ball rifled at the chimney, took a little bounce left and ended up in the centre of the narrow-left side of the fairway.

Steve took aim at the left edge of the fairway bunker and hit a nice draw into the fairway. As we walked down the fairway, he expressed his appreciation for the myofascial release techniques and can't believe how good he felt. We discussed a few protocols around the myofascial release and correct movement. I have 20 years of experience as a personal trainer and I am passionate about functional movement as opposed to most traditional gym exercises. I believe that regular functional exercise is essential to playing your best golf and living your best life.

Steve had 260 metres to the green, and the fairway ahead had two big fairway bunkers that needed to be negotiated. The pin was front right, guarded by a bunker at the front right of the green and another two bunkers greenside to the right. Ideally, Steve wanted to leave himself a shot of around 80 metres from the left side of the fairway. That would mean laying up short of the left fairway bunker, which was 30 – 40 metres short of the green. When laying up, the last thing you want to do is hit it too well and end up in the trouble you are trying to avoid, so always allow 20 metres or so in case the ball flies too far or gets a big bounce. So, Steve had 180 metres to play with. He took a 6-iron, which should travel 160 – 170 metres after runout on the fairway and not reach the bunkers. He went through his routine and hit a crisp 6-iron. It flew strongly through a light breeze, bounced, and rolled out perfectly down the left side of the fairway, about 10 metres short inside of the bunker line, thus providing a margin for error if it had bounded a lot further.

You should never aim at bunkers or hazards unless it's absolutely unavoidable. Aim as close as you must, but ideally, try to hit away from trouble and allow for the ball to come out too straight or too long. There's nothing more frustrating than aiming at a bunker and thinking, I will shape away from it, but you hit it flush and it goes dead straight into the bunker.

I approached my ball, mindful to stay in the present. I did not want to to get ahead of myself and start thinking about birdies and eagles, so I brought myself back by feeling the ground under my feet and I watched the leaves in the trees gently bend in the breeze. I reached my ball and assessed the shot. I had 235 metres to the flag, with a bunker 30 metres short and left of the green. The fairway ran back towards the green and brought the right greenside bunkers into play.

Times and shots like this require your inner guide, a mix of subconscious experience and spirit, to come together to influence your decision. Although there were several risks involved with going for the green in two, my inner guide was full of confidence. The wind was a little off to the right. I wanted to hit my shot just right of the left bunker, just short and left of the green, and let it run up onto the green. I took the time I needed to immerse myself in the shot; I knew I could only control the process. I chose to accept the result, and in that decision, I was detached from the outcome.

Given that our best golf is played by our subconscious mind and not our conscious mind, I had, in some way, given my inner guide permission to hit this shot. For the first time in years, I was fitted for new clubs. It was a game changer as I now had confidence that I had the best fit possible for me. So, I took out my new Mizuno 3-wood, knowing it gave me the capacity to hit this shot. I went through my routine, immersed in hitting a low, hard, straight 3-wood that would chase up onto the green. I felt this shot with every fibre of my being and approached it with a sense of detached confidence. One look at the starting line target, my eyes came back to the ball, my body reacted, and I followed the ball flight just as I had pictured. It was a solid hit – on target. The first bounce was low and hard, and it finished pin high, 25 feet to the left of the hole.

Steve had 87 metres to the hole – a solid 52-degree wedge. Ideally, you need to hit higher shots to front pins and lower shots to back pins. He was a little concerned with the ball getting caught up in the wind and falling short into the bunker, so he played the ball a little back in his stance to knock the flight down. Although the shot would come out a little lower, it would have enough spin to stop quickly – and it would be better to putt than to play a bunker shot. Steve came in committed to his decision and hit a solid gap wedge, which flew just left and 20 feet long of the hole. Again, he felt the freedom in his body was just giving him a little more distance. He would need to adjust to it but it is a nice problem to have.

Steve already had a couple of similar putts to this, although this one was a little shorter and quicker. He went through his routine and stroked a nice putt through a couple of subtle breaks, but he didn't quite hit it hard enough. It fell inches short for an easy tap-in par.

As I walked onto the green, I could see and feel the speed for a big-breaking left-to-right putt, which determined the line. I remember a great mentor and putting coach, Eric Lucas, explained and showed me the benefits of lagging long putts on the high side for big-breaking putts. Big-breaking putts that are hit on the low side will, on average, finish three times further away. For example, if I hit this putt at a speed to finish hole-high, it would finish one foot away on the high side, whereas the same putt missed low would finish three feet away.

My custom-made Lajosi putter felt great in my hands. I stood over the putt, I could feel its speed through my feet and hands, and with one last look down the line, I hit the putt. It moved six feet before I lifted my eyes to see it rolling as I imagined, on the right path. The ball continued to track online, moving slightly with the left-to-right slope as it slowed down. It came to rest a roll short of going in. I smiled with acceptance – it's always nice to make an eagle, but it was a very solid birdie. The sun was starting to really shine and the vibrant smell of spring weather was in the air. The course was in fantastic condition, and we both discussed how blessed we felt to be out playing golf in such great conditions.

Sage Advice on Inner Guide

- A guiding force.
- A constant companion.
- Operates congruently with your greatest desires and greatest actions.

Inner Guide

Your inner guide is a beautiful cocktail of cognitive and emotional experiences, blending emotional intelligence, subconscious intervention, instinct and spirit. This guide involves your subconscious picking up subtle cues, recognising patterns, and trusting beyond conscious reasoning. It combines intuition, which is the work of both your brain and your spirit, to provide insight and guidance.

Intuition is the recognition of something you have directly or indirectly learned or experienced. Your brain stores this information in your subconscious mind, so when a situation presents itself, you intuitively make decisions that suggest you know something is correct without consciously having an explanation for that decision.

In golf, it stands to reason that the longer you have played and the better you are, the more stored information you have to be used as intuition. The more expert you are in a given activity, the more accessible your intuition becomes.

In golf, nearly every shot you hit on the course is unique. Yet, you can have a strong feeling that goes beyond the logic of the data you have in front of you. You may intuitively sense that the ball will fly hard out of a particular lie, that there is moisture in the grass that will cause a flyer lie, or you sense that the green ahead will not hold easily due to its colour. You have previously stored information that your brain uses to match to the current situation.

Every good shot you have ever hit is stored away in your subconscious mind. Your mind can then blend a previous shot, like the one you are about to hit, with your imagination to formulate the best shot for the current situation. Your intuition filters this process and gives a feeling of confidence. The role of your subconscious is to continue the process of hitting the shot, removing conscious and technical thoughts out of the process.

Another form of guidance is spiritual direction. People have all kinds of experiences of spiritual guidance. In the Christian faith, for example, believers have the Holy Spirit as an ever-present guiding force. It's not so much that you receive direct advice from a spiritual force, more so you experience the fruits of that force, such as peace, patience, and self-control, which are nurturing grounds for intuition and inner guidance.

When you blend intentional living with intuitive, heart-led living, it can open you up to an exciting and adventurous life. Trust your intuition. Nurture and develop it to the point that it becomes a guiding light in your life, both on and off the golf course. By embracing your inner guide, you can navigate the complexities of golf with greater ease and confidence. This trust in your intuition can transform your game, allowing you to play with a sense of freedom and joy. Embrace your inner guide and let it lead you to new heights in your golfing journey and beyond.

Sage Questions on Inner Guide

1. In what ways can you better connect with your inner guide to unlock your fullest potential and live your most fulfilling life?

_____

_____

_____

_____

INNER GUIDE

2. How can you utilise your inner guide to help you utilise this guidance to play better golf?

_____
_____
_____
_____

3. Reflect on a magical time you experienced through your inner guide. What happened, and how could you experience this more often?

_____
_____
_____
_____

A Model of the Inner Guide: Seve Ballesteros

Seve Ballesteros's use of his inner guide was the greatest of any player in history. Deeply intertwined with his great imagination, Seve's inner guide was the force that brought to life the extraordinary shots he envisioned. The highlight reel of Seve's career has never grown old, but one of his most remarkable displays of inner guidance occurred during the final hole of the 1983 European Masters in Switzerland.

Standing on the 13th hole, Seve was five shots behind the leader. What followed was a display of brilliance as he birdied holes 13, 14, 15, 16, and 17. On the 18th hole, Seve's drive went astray; his 3-wood shot ended up blocked to the right, finishing seven feet from an eight-foot wall with trees in front of him. He had only enough room for a half backswing, which was further impeded by another tree. To make matters even more daunting, Seve needed to fly the ball over a resort swimming pool on the other side of the wall.

His caddie, frustrated that Seve wouldn't take the safe option, pleaded with him to chip out to safety. But Seve, trusting his inner guide, said, "No, I see the shot." There was a gap, which his caddie described as the size of a dinner plate. But Seve, unwavering in his trust, was not swayed by his caddie's doubts. He described the shot – over the wall, through the dinner plate-sized gap – and didn't even mention the pool. He only saw the ball, the gap, and it finishing near the green. He hit the perfect shot through the gap, and the ball finished only metres away from the green.

Seve was then faced with a tricky shot over a bunker to a close pin. In true Seve style, he made a difficult shot look easy. He holed it for a birdie – his sixth birdie in a row – to win the tournament. Seve's inner guide was built through an incredible imagination, through hard work that resulted in a strong self-belief, and by being a very resilient and highly self-trusting player. As Seve Ballesteros once said, "Golf is a game of instinct, but it's also a game of trust. Trust your gut, trust your swing, and most importantly, trust yourself." This quote perfectly encapsulates the essence of the inner guide – trusting the wisdom that comes from within, even when the path ahead seems uncertain.

CHAPTER 5
GRATITUDE

"Gratitude and joy are inexplicably linked. To bask in the joys of life, express your gratitude often."

Hole 5

We walked to the elevated fifth tee, a 393 metre par 4, with the tees set about 10 metres forward. It was easy to look around and feel grateful to be out playing on such a beautiful day. I looked down the fairway; it was wide, but focus is required even on broad holes.

I envisioned a soft draw, aiming at the right edge of the green in the distance. As I teed up, I felt the ball, the tee, and the ground. I was present, in the now, and right where I wanted to be. I felt the soft draw in my practice swing. I took aim and hit the draw, landing perfectly in the middle of the fairway – great tempo, and a solid strike from the centre of the club face.

Steve's practice swing looked quicker than usual, likely due to the longer hole and slight breeze. He stepped into the shot, settled over the ball, and hit a low hook left. His arms outraced his pivot, but it was just in the left rough – no major problems. As he walked off, he muttered about hating that shot. I asked him why. He looked at me, initially puzzled by the question, but then he smiled, realising there was a deeper reason behind it. The question served two purposes: it broke his cycle of negative thinking and prompted him to consider why he truly disliked that shot. It was not the shot itself, but what it represented. Often, the things we dislike trigger emotions and thoughts that go beyond the surface.

Steve quickly shifted his mindset and accepted his shot. We got to his ball and his ideal play was a low draw – the same shot he was cursing earlier. Life often works this way – what seemed like a setback could turn into an opportunity if we stayed open to the gifts in challenging moments.

Steve, now in a better state, accessed the feel for his next shot and hit the required draw, leaving him about 30 feet short right of the hole. A great result given the circumstances.

I'm left with an approach shot of 135 metres into a slight breeze, on an elevated green. A solid 8-iron, hit it a bit lower than my usual shot would skip it up to the back pin. I painted the picture in my mind – tracked the line of the ball, aimed 30 feet to the right of the pin and anticipated the breeze and lie, to draw the ball back toward the hole. I went through my routine, feeling calm and present, detached from the outcome. After all, a golf shot has little meaning in itself – it's the meaning we assign to it. I compressed the ball slightly, followed the picture in my mind – it checked up 12 feet right of the hole.

Steve faced his first uphill putt of significant distance. He walked his line, took practice strokes and hit the putt. It started well but came up a foot short. He was disappointed, but statistically, it was a tough distance to the hole, so a realistic goal would be a simple two-putt.

I assessed my putt and felt the speed in my hands. I struck it well, but it stayed less than an inch high. I remained peaceful, knowing I did all I could. It had broken my run of sub-par holes, but it didn't disrupt the blissful state I was in. We walked to the next tee through a tunnel under a road, worn over 25 years, with some graffiti that could dampen one's spirits. I chose to observe without judgement. We walked in silence, observing our surroundings. Emerging from the tunnel, I felt a breeze on my face that seemed to say, "Smile, you're alive, you're blessed, you're here to enjoy this golf course and this day."

Sage Advice on Gratitude

- Displays your divine favour.
- Magnifies the love in your heart.
- Connects souls.

Gratitude

Gratitude isn't just about acknowledging the good in your life; it's a practice that intertwines with key aspects like intention, faith, and resilience. By focusing on what you have to be grateful for, you reinforce the intentions you set, aligning your mindset with a positive outlook that makes it easier to achieve your goals. Gratitude nurtures your faith, reminding you of past blessings and victories, which in turn strengthens your belief that good things are always within reach.

Resilience, too, is deeply connected to gratitude. When faced with challenges – whether on the golf course or in life – gratitude helps you see obstacles as opportunities for growth. It shifts your focus from what's missing to what's possible, allowing you to bounce back stronger and more determined.

Taking the time to reflect on all the things you are grateful for, both while playing golf and in life, reveals the existence of abundance. Abundance goes beyond material wealth; it includes health, relationships and the freedom to play golf. These are all expressions of gratitude that enrich your experience on the course and in life.

The most impactful people in the world, like Jesus and Nelson Mandela, lived lives steeped in gratitude. Their gratitude fuelled their service to others, setting off a chain of positive emotions that empowered them and those around them. Gratitude sets in motion a similar chain reaction, enhancing your mental state, which is crucial for living your best life and playing your best golf.

Gratitude can transform adversity into opportunity. When things go wrong on the course, it's easy to slip into negativity. But by seeking out the positive

– the gift in the challenge – you strengthen your gratitude muscle and build resilience. This mindset not only helps you navigate tough situations but also enriches your overall well-being.

Sage Questions on Gratitude

1. How could you show more gratitude in your daily life?

   _____
   _____
   _____
   _____

2. What are two things that you can choose to be grateful for when you next play golf?

   _____
   _____
   _____
   _____

3. How might expressing gratitude change your perspective the next time you face a challenge on the course or in your life?

   _____
   _____
   _____
   _____

A Model of Gratitude: Jordan Spieth

Jordan Spieth is a modern-day golf star who has always expressed gratitude. He burst onto the PGA Tour scene with his first victory at just 19 years of age. Jordan often acknowledges the critical role of his family and support team in his success. He credits his parents, Shawn and Chris, and his siblings, including his sister Ellie, who has special needs, for providing a grounded and supportive environment. Jordan has spoken about how his family keeps him humble and appreciative of his blessings.

Gratitude plays a significant role in Jordan's life and career, not only for maintaining a grounded perspective but also for fuelling his resilience and mental fortitude on the course. By regularly expressing gratitude, Jordan cultivates a mindset that keeps him focused on the positives, even in the face of challenges. This perspective allows him to stay composed under pressure, bounce back from setbacks, and maintain a consistent level of performance.

Jordan displays his gratitude through the Jordan Spieth Family Foundation, which supports initiatives related to special needs, junior golf, and other associations. These acts are a great expression of the gratitude he has for his blessed life. His charitable work not only gives back to the community but also reinforces his sense of purpose beyond the golf course, providing him with additional motivation and inner strength.

Gratitude endears Jordan to many fans and fellow competitors, as it brings a perspective to his golf and life that nurtures resilience, increases his focus and self-belief, and keeps him connected to what truly matters. For Jordan, gratitude is more than just a feeling – it's a powerful tool that enhances his life and his game, helping him navigate the highs and lows of a professional golfing career with grace and confidence.

CHAPTER 6

IMAGINATION

"Imagination is limitless; its only limitation is the person using it."

Hole 6

We walked onto the sixth tee, a 148 metre par 3 over a big dam, playing into a slight breeze. The hole was on the front left of the green. I often walked onto this tee and imagined a hole in one. Bringing the imagined hole-in-one to life had a positive effect on my state of mind. My subconscious worked hard to bring my conscious belief to reality. I very rarely hit a below-standard shot on this hole due to the combination of a strong intention, great imagination, clear visualisation, and a faith that I would indeed hole out. It was a par 3 that I was yet to hole out on, but I knew I would one day, as I truly imagined and believed I would. This day though, with this tight front left pin, was a day to abide by the Decade Golf strategy.

Decade Golf, a golf company that works on golf strategy, has brought a lot to the game by helping golfers of all levels develop a strategy that is in line with their ability. By factoring in all the relevant information necessary for the best strategy – such as hazards, areas that typically lead to over-par scores, shot patterns, and personal shot biases – it becomes easy to trust the shot the strategy has produced. That trust leads to confidence.

My target was 15 feet right and long of the pin. Although it was a somewhat conservative target, it still required a committed swing with a 7-iron. I moved to the far left of the tee box, which helped set me right of the pin. I was smiling, a little excited, and simply happy to be out playing golf on a nice day with a great friend. But at this time, the shot is all that exists – this moment, this now. I trusted I could hit this shot; it sat well with me. I went through my routine and felt the shot through my whole body. I looked at the target, took aim, and settled into my posture with constant little movements heels wiggling, fingers and arms adjusting to optimal pressure. One more look at the hole, my eyes returned to the ball, the feeling in my hands heightened, and my intention was set on hitting the chosen shot out of the middle of the club, and bang – I hit it flush. It sailed off, and although I knew I had hit it flush, anything could happen. The wind could spring up; it could get a bad bounce. But I was detached from the outcome. As it was flying through the air, I continued to smile and just observe. It landed safely on the green, about 18 feet long and to the right – a smart play.

Steve hit a 6-iron, a little low and with less spin. It finished about 40 feet long, which was also a smart play. Sometimes it was far smarter to hit away from the pin to a safe target. Steve had another solid two-putt par. He was in a nice zone. We had played a fair bit of golf over the years and he had often obsessed over his swing. But in recent times, we've had some mindset coaching sessions together, and he had come to better understand the best version of himself as a golfer. He had rebuilt trust and rapport with himself after many years of negative self-talk, and he was no longer needy. He didn't need to play well to feel good about himself; he sourced that internally, not externally, and the overflow led to a freer golf game.

I had a slightly downhill 18-foot putt with what looked like a hint of a left-to-right break—about half a cup width. The putt came off the middle of my Lajosi putter so sweetly, rolling pure, end over end. It caught the left edge, spun around the back of the cup, and finished a couple of inches to the right. A very solid three!

As we walked to the 7th tee, we could see the 8th green. I always looked for pin positions around the course on upcoming holes. I've done that since I was a kid – checking out as many pin positions as I could before teeing off and then looking for others on my way around. Of course, there were always some holes that you don't get to see first, but I got what I could.

As we approached the 7th tee, Steve mentioned how different his mindset was now and how he wished he had thought like this 30 years ago. In some ways, I did too, but I also appreciated that sometimes the longer and harder the lesson, the more you learn and grow as a person.

Sage Advice on Imagination

- Imagination is the foundation of creation.
- Imagination opens pathways to instinctive play.
- Imagination fuels creativity and joy.

Imagination

Imagination is the foundation of all creation. Before anything can exist in the physical realm, it must first be conceived in the mind. Every object, invention or achievement you encounter began as a vision – a mental image. This principle is especially crucial in golf and life. Albert Einstein famously said, "Imagination is more important than knowledge." His rationale was that knowledge is finite, but imagination encompasses the entire world. This boundless creativity is what allows us to transcend limitations and achieve greatness.

In the Bible, the first attribute God reveals about Himself is His creativity. The act of creation is a testament to His boundless imagination. As beings made in His image, we too are endowed with this incredible creative power.

BEYOND THE FAIRWAYS TO FULFILMENT

Most amateur golfers approach the game with conscious thoughts, focusing on mechanics and technique. In contrast, the greatest golfers, such as Jack Nicklaus and Tiger Woods, harness the power of their subconscious minds through vivid imagination and creativity. They have often spoken about how their success in golf is deeply rooted in their imaginative abilities. Imagination opens pathways to play instinctively and fluidly, beyond the confines of conscious thought.

Imagination generates a positive emotion that resonates within the heart, empowering the hands to bring forth the envisioned creation. Consider a scenario where you face a challenging 110-metre shot from the trees. The shot requires you to keep the ball low under branches 30 metres ahead and curve it from left to right to avoid a greenside bunker. You might need to use a gripped-down 5 or 6-iron, played back in your stance, with a short, sharp, aggressive swing.

You may have never executed this exact shot before, yet through imagination, you can visualise and feel as though you've successfully performed it many times. Imagination begins with a clear picture of the desired outcome. This mental image provides the energy and confidence to take the necessary actions to bring it to fruition.

The fuel for imagination is faith – belief in the outcome you envision. From this belief, embody the mindset and actions required to achieve your goals.

Many golfers overly focus on the technical aspects of the swing. While mechanics are important, it's equally vital to cultivate your imagination. Spend time creatively practicing your short game with a variety of shots. This practice will invigorate your creativity and stimulate your performance.

Embrace your imagination, trust in your creative power, and let your subconscious guide you to greatness on the golf course.

Imagination Questions

1. What specific limiting beliefs do you hold that are limiting your ability to fully engage your imagination on the course?

   _____
   _____
   _____
   _____

2. Do you think excessive technical thoughts could be limiting your imagination on the course?

   _____
   _____
   _____
   _____

3. Given the power of imagination, how could you use your imagination to live a more fulfilling life?

   _____
   _____
   _____
   _____

Models of Imagination: Bobby Jones, Seve Ballasteros, Tiger Woods

Many golfing greats have thrilled fans with their brilliant imaginations both on and off the golf course. Three golfers who expressed great imaginations were Bobby Jones, Seve Ballesteros and Tiger Woods. These generational players led the way in creativity, bringing to life golf shots that had never been seen before.

BEYOND THE FAIRWAYS TO FULFILMENT

Bobby Jones used his great imagination through his creative style of play to become the greatest amateur golfer in the history of the game. His thirteen major championships are only exceeded by Jack Nicklaus and Tiger Woods. Bobby Jones expressed his imagination and gifted the golf world when he designed and co-founded the beautiful Augusta National Golf Club and the US Masters Tournament.

Watch Seve playing the 1976 British Open as a 19-year-old. He hit the ball into places no other players went, yet his imagination and creativity kept finding the answers and the shots to keep him in contention, eventually tying for second place.

Remember Tiger's famous chip-in on the par-3, 16th hole at Augusta National? He let his imagination formulate a tournament-winning shot. You could see him initially close his eyes, imagining a shot from the edge of the rough that would come out low, aimed 25 feet left of the hole, chipped up into the green's slope, then slowly released downhill into the hole. His imagination sparked his visualisation, creating the exact image of the shot, and the visualisation enabled his body to create the swing required to produce a memorable shot.

All these players had great work ethics. The power of imagination not only enhanced their games but also brought them great joy and fulfilment in their practice. Their imaginations stimulated their focus and attention that energised them to sustain long hours of practice. A great imagination is void of judgement; it's void of the falsehood of perfection. It opens a doorway to safely pursuing greatness.

These players imagined a shot, then created a neural pathway to get their bodies to produce the shot. They tried, they learned, they tried again, and eventually, they produced. They understood that there is a learning process – a path of mastery – before they could execute new shots consistently and competently. These players have great touch and feel, which is a by-product of their minds and bodies building a great relationship through the process of imagination.

CHAPTER 7
VISUALISATION

"If you can't see it, you can't be it."

Hole 7

The seventh hole was a 363 metre par 4. It featured a generously wide fairway that narrowed as you approached the green within 100 metres. The green was heavily bunkered with multiple tiers, protecting it from easy birdies. The wide fairway could sometimes lure you into reducing your focus and intentions. The great Ben Hogan often walked golf courses backwards. By backwards, I mean he started on the 18th green and walked down the fairway to the tee, continuing this way for all 18 holes. You could gain a clear perspective of the course by doing this, and often players built their course strategy by playing the hole backwards in their mind.

As I stood on the tee, I visualised playing the hole backwards to work out the best strategy. I saw where the pin was. From there, I saw the best part of the fairway to approach that pin. Then, I selected the best side of the tee box to set me up towards that ideal position on the fairway. From behind the ball on the tee, I visualised playing my tee shot to match the best strategy for the hole. This brought certainty, which strengthened self-belief and confidence. With a clear plan in mind, I could approach my shot with a calm focus, knowing exactly what I wanted to achieve and trusting in my ability to execute the plan.

My routine has two zones. The assessment zone, where I stand behind the ball and articulate to myself the shot I am going to hit, then I visualise and feel the shot. I tug my shirt over my left shoulder and step in towards the ball. Once I walk in, I focus on my aim, look at the target and swing thought-free, as detached from the outcome as possible.

As I teed up my ball, I was mindful to really feel the ball, the tee, and the ground to ensure I was in the moment, where life's magic manifested. I felt absolutely present and felt so free. I went through my routine and hit the shot just as I had pictured. It felt pure but effortless, and it landed in the perfect position.

Steve stood behind the ball with his eyes closed for a moment, visualising his shot. He made a couple of practice swings that looked like he was trying to hit a little fade, the opposite shape to the hook he hit on his drive back on the fifth hole. He then walked into the ball, but he looked almost a little hesitant. He made a slightly tentative swing and hit a little cut against the breeze that finished on the right edge of the fairway. Steve had 142 metres to the hole and hit a 7-iron. Again, he looked a little hesitant, and his shot leaked off to the right edge of the green.

I had 90 metres to the hole. A three-quarter 53-degree wedge would be perfect. I aimed to hit it 91 metres and expected a little backspin. The shot that was set up nicely for me – very straightforward. I aimed a metre left of the hole and made a committed swing. The fairways are Santa Ana Couch grass and had pretty tight lies. You needed to compress the ball with these fairways. I intended to make a fairly aggressive but controlled three-quarter swing to spin it back a little. My aim was good, and the contact felt solid. I could feel the ball catch the perfect groove on my club, and the flight of the ball matched the shot. It bounced just left and past the hole, it spun back, missing the right side, and came to rest a metre below the hole.

Most tour professionals have an almost perfect percentage from three feet, but some certainly have their challenges over this distance. I recall a time I felt uncomfortable over that range, but thankfully, those days are long gone. Once I worked out my ideal eye line for putting, which for me was slightly inside the ball, and then matched my stroke mechanics to that, I had my ideal profile path – this was the great work of Bruce Rearick of Burnt Edges Putting. From there, once fitted for my Lajosi putter, which matched my profile, it was happy days. I certainly do the required quality practice. That, coupled with a healthy amount of confidence, made for good putting.

Steve bunted a little rescue chip shot, which was a great shot when faced with grainy greenside chips. It came to rest less than a foot short and left of the hole – a stress-free 4. I cleaned my ball, replaced it, stood behind the putt, took two practice strokes to gain feel, aimed left centre of the hole and hit a solid putt from the sweet spot of the putter into the hole. We walked off the green, and I said to Steve, "You're playing solid golf, just enjoy it and stay in the now." He smiled like a 12-year-old being praised.

I think it's innate that humans like encouragement. We seem to have lost our way in this tech-crazy world that seeks to reward anyone who puts up a self-proclaiming post. Often we praise and applaud anything on social media yet forget to celebrate our children getting to the next level of their reading and spelling or acing a math test. Give authentic praise and encouragement where it's due, and perhaps less on social media to people you have never met.

Sage Advice on Visualisation

- Visualisation is a key link from intention to a desired outcome.
- Visualisation aligns your mind and body.
- Visualisation turns dreams into reality.

Visualisation

Since the dawn of time, visualisation has been the bridge between imagination and physical manifestation. People have envisioned things yet unseen – like buildings, cars, planes and phones – transforming mental images into tangible realities. In the realm of golf, visualisation sharpens focus and directs attention to enhance desired outcomes. It is a crucial tool for any golfer aiming for excellence.

Visualisation allows you to mentally rehearse a desired outcome before the actual performance, preparing you for different potential scenarios. This mental practice can evoke both physical and emotional sensations, enhancing the vividness of your mental images. By incorporating sensory attributes like sight, sound, touch, smell, and taste, visualisation deepens belief and clarifies intentions. These emotions drive the necessary actions to turn visualised scenarios into physical experiences.

Your mind shapes your reality. The clearer the picture of your desired outcome, the greater the chance of achieving it. For golfers, visualisation can be a game-changer. Picture an upcoming round or tournament: see the course, imagine playing a great round, picture the drive to the course, and mentally rehearse your warm-up routine. Focus particularly on key shots, like your first drive or the final hole. The more detailed and frequent your visualisations, the more you set yourself up for success. This mental rehearsal brings certainty and comfort, making the actual experience feel familiar and achievable.

Visualisation not only sharpens your focus but also sets strong intentions. Attention follows intention, and where attention goes, energy flows. This energy is channelled into actions; for instance, if you visualise your game at a level beyond your current ability, your subconscious will nudge you to practice more, refine your skills, or enhance your fitness. The belief formed through visualisation drives these positive behaviours, creating a feedback loop of improvement.

VISUALISATION

People often go through the motions of visualising a shot when playing. However, there are levels to the intensity of visualisation. You can casually imagine hitting a shot somewhere near the flag, or you can enhance your visualisation by seeing and feeling the trajectory of the ball's flight, how it lands and reacts on the green, and even the side and speed at which the ball enters the hole. The more vivid and detailed your visualisation, the stronger it will morph into the swing feel required to produce that great shot you have envisioned.

Visualising can also create a powerful sense of déjà vu. When you experience what you've repeatedly visualised – be it practice sessions or competitive rounds – you feel as though you've already accomplished it. This familiarity breeds confidence and calm, reinforcing the belief that you can achieve your goals.

Enhance your visualisations by imagining every detail: the clothes you wear, the language you use, the food you eat, and the person you are. Engaging all your senses in these mental rehearsals amplifies the power of visualisation, making the imagined scenario more real and attainable.

Incorporating visualisation into your golf routine can transform your mindset and performance. By seeing success in your mind's eye, you pave the way for its reality. This mental practice is not just about imagining; it's about believing, preparing, and ultimately, achieving your golfing aspirations.

Sage Questions on Visualisation

1. Can you recall a time in your life when you successfully used visualisation to achieve a desired outcome? What was the experience like?

_____
_____
_____
_____

2. Visualisation can manifest as mental images or physical sensations. How do you incorporate visualisation into your pre-shot routine in golf?

_____
_____
_____
_____

3. What specific outcomes do you desire in your life or golf that, through the practice of visualisation, could help achieve your goals?

_____
_____
_____
_____

A Model of Visualisation: Jack Nicklaus

The great visualisers of the game have always displayed a steely focus. Jack Nicklaus, the greatest major winner of all time, was also one of the greatest visualisers of all time. He never hit a putt until he could first visualise the ball going in. At times, he seemed to stand over a putt for a long time, but until he was convinced it was going in, he wouldn't strike the putt. Jack attributed his visualisation techniques to his mentor and coach, Jack Grout, who worked on the importance of the mental game and visualisation, in addition to physical practice.

Before every shot, Nicklaus would go through a meticulous routine of visualisation. He didn't just see the shot; he felt it. He would visualise the entire trajectory, from the ball's initial flight to its landing, and even how it would roll out. This intense focus and clarity allowed him to execute with remarkable consistency under pressure.

One of the most famous examples of his visualisation in action was during the 1972 US Open at Pebble Beach. Facing the 17th hole, with the wind howling and a treacherous pin position, Nicklaus visualised the perfect 1-iron shot. He saw the ball cutting through the wind, landing just short of the green, and bouncing up to nestle near the hole. His visualisation was so vivid that when he struck the shot, it played out exactly as he had seen it in his mind, leading to one of the most iconic moments in golf history.

Nicklaus's legacy as a master of visualisation has influenced countless golfers, demonstrating how mental preparation can be just as crucial as physical skill. His ability to visualise every detail of his shots contributed to his unparalleled success, especially in the high-pressure moments that define greatness.

CHAPTER 8
ACCOUNTABILITY

"Accountability is the empowering choice to own your decisions, actions and outcomes."

Hole 8

Standing on the eighth tee, a 535 metre par 5, the ancient sage had the fairway bunkering arranged in a manner that suggested you hit down the left side and make the hole play its length. But with the breeze helping slightly from the left and trusting my driving ability, I decided on a riskier line, right of centre that required a longer bunker carry. It took two good shots to reach the green; but it was a calculated risk that I was confident I could pull off. And with 100 percent commitment, I hit a great shot that finished just right of centre and gave me a good angle into the green.

Steve went through his routine, and I sensed he was in a sweet zone himself. His practice swing looked strong and free. He aimed a little left of mine to a wider, safer part of the fairway. The swing had great tempo, and he really crunched it down the left centre of the fairway. He couldn't reach the green in two from where he was, so he hit a three wood down the right centre to a great spot that left a straightforward wedge to the hole.

I had 240 metres to the hole. My starting line over was a large fairway bunker about 90 metres short of the green. There was a flagpole behind the green that

I used as my sightline, as the hole was blinded by the fairway bunker. I took a practice swing, just letting my subconscious prepare my body for what was required. Once I had chosen the shot, talked it through with myself, and primed my body with a practice swing, it was now time for my mind to quieten down.

Self-talk and a check-list of all our swing thoughts when standing over the ball will inevitably result in a poor shot. By playing golf with our subconscious mind and not our conscious mind will lead to our best shots. Imagine standing over the ball, and someone said, "Righto, make sure your aim's correct, get your grip right, tuck your bum in a little, one-piece takeaway, soft hands, make sure it's pivot-driven," and on and on… It would drive you bonkers – you wouldn't enjoy it or expect to hit a great shot.

So, as I walked into the shot, to quieten my mind, I repeated the number nine over and over in my brain. I aligned my club to the right edge of a fairway bunker 90 metres short of the green. I aligned my feet and body, took one last look at the target, and saying a long number nine to myself, I swung freely and strongly. I felt the strong, crisp strike out of the centre of my new Mizuno 3-wood. It flew sweetly to the right edge of the bunker, the outcome unknown because of a very large bunker lip. Barring an obscure bounce, the ball should be on or close to the flag on the bottom tier of the green, which I had seen when I was on the 7th tee.

Steve had wisely played right of the bunker that left him a 70 metre pitch shot, which is his favourite length. We worked together on his wedge game – a combination of technical improvements around his setup including levelling out his previously over-tilted shoulders, improving his pivot and arm sequence and practicing scoring drills, this meant he can now pitch it to a scratch marker's level. He looked committed and comfortable over this shot. We made a rule that you must be 100 percent committed to the shot you are standing over, and if that commitment breaks at any stage, you must back away from the shot and restart your routine. Steve pitched it about 10 feet short of the hole; it took a skip and finished 3 feet short and right of the hole. His childish grin appeared,

ACCOUNTABILITY

and his demeaner was noticeably better than it was after his 5th tee shot. He had a long history of being very critical of himself, but we had made massive inroads since working on his mindset.

I love the creativity available in the short game; seeing pictures of the shot, creating the feel for that shot, and then bringing it to life. Growing up playing a variety of courses, I found it beneficial to be able to chip with pretty much every club from a 4-iron to a lob wedge. Some people prefer to mainly use their sand wedge – I believe you should use what works best for you.

My ball was a metre short of the green, and I had about 20 feet to the hole with a slightly left-to-right break. I read this chip as a putt and wanted to get it rolling on the green as soon as possible. It was a simple process from seeing, feeling, and hitting the shot. I took my setup, aware of the softness in my hands, detached from the outcome. Using a 9-iron, I looked at the target, looked back at the ball, and without a thought, I chipped it two metres and it ran out like a putt. It felt good, looked great halfway, lost a little speed and finished inches to the right. A simple tap-in birdie.

Without much fuss, Steve went through his putting routine from behind the ball, he walked in and made his solid birdie four.

It is important to maintain your optimal state so having uplifting conversations during golf can help. It was a bit of a walk to the 9th tee, so we started talking about the Geelong Cats, the Australian rules football team — Steve's beloved AFL football team. They had arguably been the most consistent club for the past 20 years. They seemed to have a great community culture, quality individuals with sound morals and ethics, and good coaching staff who have great strategies and flexibility in their game plan. I also like the Cats as my darling Mum has been a lifelong supporter. We approached the 9th tee with good vibes.

Sometimes when you have played a hole so well and without much conscious thought, you wonder how it could ever be complicated. But unfortunately, sometimes, or for some people all the time, we get our insecure, overbearing conscious minds involved and cramp our own style, restricting our true ability.

Sage Advice on Accountability

- Accountability is the commitment to excellence, the discipline to improve, and the courage to own your journey.
- Accountability demonstrates great strength of character and security.
- The overflow of accountability is a person who is trustworthy, respected and at peace with their efforts and outcomes.

Accountability

Accountability is a fundamental requirement for success in both golf and life. It means taking full ownership of your actions and their consequences. The quality of your golf game and your life is largely determined by the thoughts and actions you are accountable for. Winners embrace accountability, assessing their actions and outcomes, learning from the results, and growing from the experience.

A golfer must be accountable for different aspects including understanding their swing technique and recognising their swing and game tendencies. Accountability extends to preparation, which encompasses mental, physical, and technical readiness. Equally important is managing emotional resilience and stress levels on and off the course. A golfer should also be diligent in setting and reviewing goals, maintaining equipment, and nurturing a healthy lifestyle that supports peak performance. By taking responsibility for these elements, a golfer can build a solid foundation for consistent improvement and success.

By taking ownership of your outcomes, you build confidence in your ability to influence the results you desire. A high level of self-awareness enhances accountability, with reflection and assessment crucial tools in the pursuit of excellence. When you are clear about your goals and have developed strategies to achieve them, accountability involves tracking your progress through data, statistics, or accountability partners. Most professional golfers analyse data and statistics from their rounds to identify areas for improvement. Without awareness of what's holding you back, achieving your desired outcomes is nearly impossible.

Being accountable often means confronting your insecurities. You can no longer hide behind them; you must face the untruths that form your insecurities and deal with them directly. These insecurities often stem from childhood misunderstandings, leading you to outsource blame to avoid personal responsibility. However, by outsourcing blame, you also forfeit the opportunity to learn and grow.

Instead of blaming slow, bumpy greens for poor putting, take responsibility. Analyse your actions to understand your results. Perhaps you used an old ball, which statistically has a lower chance of going in the hole than a new one. Maybe you were gripping the putter too tightly, or your tempo was off. By embracing accountability, you find the path to improvement.

Along this path, you will build resilience through continued effort, driven by a love for mastery and the process of growth. You will develop a high level of trust and confidence in yourself, knowing that you are fearlessly pursuing your best, free from fear and doubt, thanks to your commitment to accountability.

Accountability transforms challenges into opportunities and setbacks into lessons. It is the cornerstone of a strong mindset, empowering you to achieve your highest potential both in golf and life. Embrace it and watch your game – and your life – elevate to new heights.

Sage Questions on Accountability

1. In what specific areas of your golf game and personal life have you been avoiding responsibility, and how can taking full ownership of these areas transform your performance and outcomes?

_____
_____
_____
_____

2. What are the underlying insecurities or fears that prevent you from being fully accountable, and how can addressing these insecurities directly lead to personal growth and improved performance on and off the course?

_____
_____
_____
_____

3. What methods or tools can you implement to consistently track your progress and stay committed to your goals in golf and life? How will you measure success and adapt your strategies to ensure continuous improvement and achievement?

_____
_____
_____
_____

A Model of Accountability: Annika Sörenstam

The great Swedish professional Annika Sörenstam is highly regarded for her professionalism and integrity on and off the course. She held herself to a very high standard. She was thorough in her regular assessments of her game and meticulous in practice and tournament preparation. She was always very open and honest in all aspects of her golf and life.

One of her great acts of accountability and honesty came on the 10th hole in the final round of a US Open, which she was leading. Her ball moved slightly in the rough; she called a penalty on herself and lost the tournament. Annika, like many highly successful people who are very accountable for their actions, was very focused, very driven, always accepted responsibility, and was humble in victory and graceful in defeat. She was very resilient and admired greatly for the way she carried herself both on and off the golf course.

CHAPTER 9
TRUST

"The essential ingredient to living your best life."

Hole 9

The ninth hole was a 364 metre par 4. A well-placed fairway bunker down the right side, bunkers greenside left and right, and a deep valley at the front right side of the green make for a tough up-and-down.

Standing on the ninth tee, we were both smiling, both enjoying ourselves. The gentle left-to-right breeze communicated that a strong, soft fading tee shot off the left side of the fairway would feed down a big embankment to the right centre. I felt it was a shot that matched what I saw. I used the middle of the tee ground as it gave me the best feel for that shot.

Sometimes, if you tee the ball too far on the right side, it can set you up to hit it left; conversely, if you tee the ball on the left side, it can set you up too far to the right. The middle ground sets me up comfortably. Assessment and swing priming done, I walked in saying 9-9-9, going through my setup routine, then a long nine as I launched a great drive perfectly flighted down the left side of the fairway, where it kicked right, a long way down.

Steve followed a similar line but just caught the ball a little low on the clubface, which took a fair amount of distance off his shot, but no harm was done, his ball was in the middle of the fairway. Steve was left with a 7-iron into the green, a little left-to-right down breeze shot. He struck it nicely – though perhaps misaligned to the right – it landed on the edge of the green and kicked right into the greenside valley.

I had 110 metres to the pin, just a very easy wedge. I felt good over the shot and the swing felt effortless, but the ball flew over the pin, a good 20 feet long. Sometimes you just catch a shot too well, you are a little bit too pumped up, or you simply just swing it with such a great sequence that it produces a little extra power. Initially, I was a little surprised, but a wry smile conveyed my acceptance, and it was time to move on.

The irony of golf is that sometimes you hit a great shot close to the hole, only to miss the putt. Other times, you hit a below standard shot far from the hole but make the putt. Adopting a mindset like "This next shot is an opportunity to do something special" or "All things work out for my good" can be powerful ways to overcome less-than-ideal shots and stay positive.

Back to the tricky greenside valley shot. Steve had to pitch up to an elevated green. The hole was centred, so he had a bit of room to land his shot. He hit a nice, crisp pitch that landed a little short. It gripped really quickly, leaving him a slightly uphill putt with a cup-width right to left break – a testy 12-foot putt for par. He looked confident and committed, and with very little fuss, he went through his routine and struck a great putt into the middle of the hole. He walked assertively to pick up the ball and gave a little laugh that said, "Gee, that felt good."

My putt had a tricky double break. The little right-to-left at the start was not as influential as the little left-to-right at the end. If the breaks were similar in size and slope, the start where the ball was rolling faster would be less affected by the slope, while the ball rolling moving more slowly at the end would be more affected. I wasn't 100 percent sure of the putt, and with this doubt, hit a slightly weak putt that finished a foot short. It never really had a chance, but it was an easy tap-in 4.

TRUST

You usually strike a putt better when you are fully trusting and committed, but golf is not a game of perfection. It's about making the best choice you can at that given time, being wholehearted in your effort, and accepting and learning from the outcome.

Sage Advice on Trust

- Trust is the root of which confidence is the fruit.
- Trust is fuelled by faith, doubt is fuelled by fear.
- Being impeccable with your word is a fundamental requirement of trust.

Trust

Trust is a fundamental to success and fulfilment. Every meaningful relationship in your life is built on trust. Having a high level of trust and rapport with oneself is essential to playing your best golf and living your best life.

Trust in sport has different forms and layers. At a basic level, it's about doing the reps required to build a skill that holds up under pressure – a skill you can trust. It's essential to have a comprehensive understanding of your game. Know your swing technique, your tendencies, and your strengths and your weaknesses. This awareness not only highlights areas for improvement, but also aids in formulating effective gameplay strategies. There is no substitute for hard work. The greats of golf have always said the secret is in the dirt. They practiced so mindfully that they developed profound trust and understanding of their games – something that could only be achieved through long hours of dedicated practice.

But trust goes beyond skill competency; it delves into the heart of self-belief and emotional resilience. To trust yourself is to believe deeply that, no matter the outcome, you have the strength and the ability to handle whatever life throws your way. This belief is forged in moments of adversity, when your resolve is tested, and it is here that trust becomes more than just a concept – it becomes your foundation.

Think of all the times you've faced doubt, both on and off the course. In those moments, trust is the voice that quiets the noise of insecurity and fear. It's the confidence that allows you to stand over a crucial putt or make a tough life decision, knowing that whatever happens, you'll be OK. Trust isn't just about hitting a shot or making a decision; it's about believing that you have what it takes to navigate the consequences of that shot or decision, whether it brings victory or challenge.

How do you rebuild trust and rapport when it's been broken? You apologise to yourself. If there are times you feel you have let yourself down and broken rapport, you will be required to go back and apologise. Life isn't about being the perfect person – that's a cruel pursuit – but it is about being authentic and wholehearted.

Apologise to yourself and understand how letting yourself down has had a flow-on effect. The apology should encompass an understanding of why you let yourself down, acknowledging how it felt and having a strategy to prevent it from happening in the future. Now, it may be a strange concept to apologise to yourself if you have never done it, but it's certainly life changing.

Imagine in a friendship or relationship that someone had done something to you that betrayed your trust. The only way to truly repair that trust would be to receive and accept an apology. Or imagine you were in some type of relationship where you were regularly mistreated, and there was never an apology. Such a relationship would have so much broken rapport that it would become very dysfunctional. That is what happens when you betray your own trust and lose rapport with yourself. You become more dysfunctional and restrict your ability to do your best.

The overflow of trust and rapport is that you remove a lot of friction that can often hold you back from being your best. Trust brings about confidence that you have the capacity to handle the consequences of your desired outcome, irrespective of it being a positive or negative outcome. If it's positive, I win – otherwise, I learn. This deep-seated confidence in your ability to learn and grow, even from setbacks, is what turns trust into a superpower.

Trust can also be broken through a misunderstanding. Often, the limiting beliefs that are currently holding you back are a childhood misunderstanding. Something occurred that led you to losing trust in yourself. If you were to go back and review what happened, you would most likely find that the disempowering accusations you made are untrue. It's simply a misunderstanding, and if you evaluate the evidence, you could see the truth and restore the trust.

For example, a golfer can have a day where they have multiple three putts. Usually, the player is a good putter, but they have a below-standard day, and suddenly they accuse themselves of being a poor putter. This judgement becomes a belief, and in a short time, this belief plays out as poor putting. Trust was broken because a story was allowed to run rampant and then caused adverse flow-on effects. Had the putting been reviewed systematically, it may have been that ball position was too far forward, which caused the ball to start further left of the target than usual. A simple adjustment to the ball position would have resulted in the usual solid standard of putting, and trust and confidence could easily be maintained.

Being impeccable with your word and being a person true to their word is the beginning and an absolute necessity for trusting oneself. From there, you build the necessary pathways to the success you seek.

Whether it's on the golf course over a tee shot or a putt, or in another area of your life, to achieve something of great significance to you, you are going to have to trust yourself like never before. Now is the time to be ready for when that moment comes. You need to honestly know in your heart and soul that you trust yourself 100 percent.

Sage Questions on Trust

1. Are you consistently true to your word? In what ways could you improve to ensure your actions align with your commitments?
   _____
   _____
   _____
   _____

2. Do you have complete trust in yourself as a person? If not, what steps can you take to strengthen that trust?
   _____
   _____
   _____
   _____

3. In which aspects of your game do you want to build a deeper level of trust, and how can you work towards achieving this?
   _____
   _____
   _____
   _____

A Model of Trust: Ben Hogan

Ben Hogan, the man who largely shaped the modern-day golf swing, displayed an incredible amount of trust in himself throughout his golf career and his life. He battled to make a living financially for the first decade of his career, but he believed he had the talent – he had a vision that one day he would be one of the greatest golfers to ever play the game. His mastery of and dedication to his golf swing enabled him to develop an incredible trust in his ability to hit remarkable shots under major pressure.

Hogan famously only played one British Open, the 1953 Open at Carnoustie, where he took a line on the 18th hole that would famously be coined "Hogan's Alley". He threaded his tee shots on the 18th fairway between out-of-bounds on the left and two fairway bunkers on the right of his line. This line was instrumental in him birdieing the last hole of the tournament to eventually win by four shots.

Another legacy-making shot was Hogan's famous 1-iron shot into the 18th hole at Merion Golf Club to win the 1950 US Open. He had built so much trust in his swing through a dedication to mastery and the pursuit of excellence – not perfection – that the greater the pressure, the better he felt he performed. Hogan often said, "The secret is in the dirt," but no matter how much he practiced, if he did not trust himself and his game the way he did, he would not have achieved what he did. His trust in himself was a superpower – rooted not only in his skill but in the unshakeable belief that he could face any challenge and emerge stronger for it.

CHAPTER 10
TRANSITION SPACE

"A beautiful space in which you can reflect, reset, refocus, and again be your best in the next space."

Hole 10

Golf can often feel like a game of two nines. Ideally, it should flow as a continuum of present moments, with brief reset spaces in between. However, many golfers use the 10th tee as a time to re-energise with a drink and a snack and to tally up their score. This practice can be detrimental, as it shifts the focus to the score rather than maintaining immersion in a good process.

The key to the tenth tee space, as you transition into your second nine, is to maintain or enter your optimal state. Reset your focus to the next shot only, avoiding the temptation to mentally predict the next nine holes. Take a breath, reset, and hit a great drive on hole number 10.

The tenth hole, a 408-metre par 4, could play brutally long into a winter's northerly wind or quite short with a summer's easterly side wind. The slight easterly made it play a little easier. A slightly sweeping right-to-left fairway, with a light right-to-left breeze, made it easy to feel and execute a right-to-left tee shot. I chose a line down the right side of the fairway. In my assessment zone behind the ball, I was crystal clear about the shot and fully trusted that I would hit it. Once I took that first step into the ball, my vocal conscious mind knew that it was no longer required and was quiet. My subconscious, through the work of the cerebellum, was in charge now. Some quiet number 9s were repeated as I walked in and kept the calm and capable cerebellum in charge. I set the club to the starting line and my body to the club. I took one last look, then swung away. A swing of freedom with no conscious thoughts. The impact was both hard and light, and the ball rocketed off like it had been programmed by the world's most sophisticated computer – and it had – the mind. It was the perfect shot that left me feeling grateful and content.

Steve aimed down the centre of the fairway and swung a little out to the right on his through swing, which caused the ball to go left with a draw. It was just off the fairway in the light rough.

Often, people who draw the ball too much will compensate by swinging out to the right. It is a logical thing to do, but golf's not always logical – you actually need to swing to the left to stop the ball going left. Picture someone who has a big slice: they aim left, swing hard left, and the ball cuts off to the right.

The hole was positioned short left on the front of the green behind a cluster of bunkers. Steve had 154 metres to the pin, but it was a red light shot, which means choose a safer target. As he was coming out of the rough, there would be no spin and as he was hitting to a slightly elevated green, the ball would come in with less height. He had to fly a cluster of deep bunkers, which would short side him, meaning he would have little green to work with if his shot ended in the bunker. His best option was to aim well away from the hole.

Steve took aim at the front right of the green. He hit a 7-iron, anticipating it would go about 145 metres to his chosen target. He was totally committed and made a solid swing. The ball came out quite hard as expected, hit a slight upslope before the green, and finished in the perfect position about one metre off the green, short right, leaving a straightforward uphill chip or putt.

I had 142 metres to the hole. I chose to use the wind rather than fight it – a slight breeze off the right in the spring air – this was a smooth 8-iron. I was mindful not to get too aggressive with my target. There was plenty of green to the right of the hole, and it was a straightforward putt. The green slopes back to front, and this shot had the potential to spin or at least stop quickly.

Using an internal target gauge, I picked a tight target – in this case, the pin, but my gauge said no, it was a little too aggressive. I then chose a very conservative target to the right – no, too wide, I didn't feel a connection to that target. I settled on a target three metres right of the pin that felt perfect for my gauge. The likelihood was that, based on my shot pattern with my 8-iron, it may finish slightly left of my target. I went through my pre-shot routine, fully engaged, and committed to my target. My practice swings felt smooth and my body was ready for this shot. I settled into the ball, looked at the target, then back to the ball, and without hesitation, whack. The shot was right out of the middle of the club, on the lower grooves of the centre. It was going to land like a butterfly with sore feet. I could almost see it spinning in the air; it landed two metres right of the pin and two metres short, took a bounce, and stopped dead, four feet from the hole.

Steve had a very straightforward, uphill shot with a little right-to-left break; he just needed the right speed. There were many shots he could play, but it was a very into-the-grain lie, which could be tricky. I often use a rescue club with a putting action from this type of lie and I suggested he do the same. A couple of practice strokes, and he rolled it up to a foot, grabbed his putter, and tapped in his par putt.

I had a four-foot, slightly uphill. Every putt is really a straight putt, but our aim points vary. I had a small breaking uphill right-to-left putt. I went through my routine, stayed in the now, and calmly rolled the ball into the centre of the cup. As we strolled to the 11th tee, we felt the breeze drying out, and the fragrance of spring becoming stronger. I had always loved the smell of spring; I think of it as the precursor to those warm summer days that I absolutely love playing golf in.

Sage Advice on Transition Space

- Be very intentional about who you need to be when transitioning from one space to the next.
- Transitioning correctly is good for you, it's helpful for the people you deal with, and therefore, it's beneficial for the world.
- The transition space is a great place to decompress, reflect, learn, grow, refocus, re-energise and re-set.

Transition Space

The speed at which you live now is faster than it's ever been, but it's also the slowest it will ever be. People seem to wear "busy" as a badge of honour and are forever in a hurry. Imagine if Superman didn't transition properly – he would not be his best Clark Kent and an even worse Superman.

When you come to the golf course, you are transitioning from somewhere. It may be from your home life as a partner, a parent, or a home worker. You may be coming from your workplace or from a place of study – you are transitioning from somewhere.

Reflect, if necessary, on where you have come from. Take in all the relevant reflective information. Process it as best you can, and if further reflection is required, tell yourself you will park it mentally for now – you will disconnect from it, and reconnect and address it later. Once you have reflected, breathe, and bring yourself to the now. It's very important to clean the space you're about to enter, which in this case is the golf course. Look around and be aware of where you are physically and mentally. Then set your intentions for the next space, the golf course. Your intentions will attract your attention, and where attention goes, energy flows.

The transition space for golf should include some breathing exercises or forms of meditation. The breath is a great anchor to the present. The breath will help bring you calmly back to yourself. There are many types of breathing exercises. Box breathing is a nice starting place. You take a four-second breath in, hold for four seconds, exhale for four seconds, hold for four seconds, and repeat a few times. Do it in a safe environment.

Golf requires great focus and state control – the ability to get yourself into an optimal emotional state and maintain it for four to five hours. It's not about sustaining an intense focus, but more about setting the thermostat of your attitude and emotions and maintaining it within ideal parameters. On the golf course, you can create a space before the shot – the pre-shot routine – to prepare yourself both mentally and physically for the shot ahead. After the shot, you can create a space where you give yourself 10 seconds or so to reflect it, process the outcome, then reset for the next shot. That process may be marked by the time between when you hit the shot, your processing space, and putting your club back in your bag.

The same goes for transitioning from golf to your next activity or space. Take the time to reflect on your round. Be grateful that you were able to play. Then, clean the space to enable you to transition. You often have different avatars of yourself in different settings. It's important when you transition, like Superman, that you fully transition. This may require a shower and a change of clothes, breath work, meditation, a gym workout – whatever it may be – so you can successfully transition to the next space as the best version of you.

Remember, show up at your best when it matters most. This requires awareness and preparation. When you create space, you expand time; when you expand time, you create a place to breathe, and your breath is the essence of your life.

Sage Questions on Transition Space

1. How can you create smoother transitions between the different spaces in your life to achieve your optimal state?

   _____
   _____
   _____
   _____

2. Do you have any rituals that help you transition effectively from one space to another? If not, what practices could you implement to improve these transitions?

   _____
   _____
   _____
   _____

3. Can you describe your mental and physical approach when transitioning from one shot to the next?

   _____
   _____
   _____
   _____

A Model of Transition Space: Jack Nicklaus

It's both incredible and interesting that Jack Nicklaus is arguably the greatest player of all time, one of the biggest golf player brands, and the best user of transition space both on and off the golf course.

Jack's consistent and deliberate pre-shot routine helped him transition smoothly from one shot to the next. His ability to transition so well between shots throughout his entire career showcased his strategic mind, emotional control, and adaptability.

Jack's transition skills were also very evident in the way he prioritised his family, including raising five children and maintaining a close-knit family. Several times, Jack would fly out from a tournament for an evening to attend a family function, only to return late that night or early the next morning to reconvene his tournament play. His ability to transition from building a business empire to being a great family man, commentator, golf course designer, and during many of those times, still a world-class tournament golfer, is a testament to his great ability to transition. It also underscores the power of utilising transition space effectively and the great benefits it brings.

CHAPTER 11
THE NOW

"The now is a fleeting experience comparable to the joy and peace of eternity."

Hole 11

Living in the now and practicing mindfulness have become very in vogue in this current day. I think the now is more a term of endearment toward time rather than an actuality. The time we live in is an oscillation between the past and the future. I think the closest we get to living in the now is when we experience time with no conscious or recognisable thoughts or emotions of our past or future. But using the word as it's used in society today, being in the now is a key fundamental to experiencing peak performance.

There have been strategies to play your golf round in 3-hole blocks or one hole at a time, but great golf is played one shot at a time. That one shot is played in the now.

There is no better place to hang out than in the now. There is never a shortage of now, and now is the only place you can do things. There is no need to load up the now – this now is sufficient and perfect. This now is where the true magic and fulfilment of life and golf exist. Not in the past, not in the future, but right here and now. And as those perfect moments continue without separation, you will enjoy the manifestation of your heart's desires.

The eleventh hole was a 169 metre par 3 with a long, narrow green. This day, the wind was from the left, with the pin on the back tier, guarded tightly by a pot bunker to the left. The middle of the green was always a good spot to be on this hole, especially with a back left hole. Although the wind could move the ball a touch further right, it was the best strategy to use on this hole. Knowing your distances with all your clubs is something that most people are aware of, but knowing your shot patterns and dispersion patterns is just as important.

I teed the ball in the middle of the tee ground, aiming at the middle of the green, just right of the pin. A solidly struck shot would not move too much in this breeze. A strong, uncomplicated 6 iron was my shot. I did a swing to prime my body and a routine to clean my mental space. I walked in with a quiet mind, aimed my club to my target, put my body to the club, and maintained a great softness through my body - a look at the target, a look at the ball, and I hit it. Solid. It felt effortless. The ball flew off with a wind-piercing flight, barely affected. It landed around my 156 metre 6 iron carry distance and settled about 24 feet right of the pin.

Steve chose a 5 iron and followed my lead; he used the middle of the tee and aimed at the middle of the green. He seemed like he was settling into his round, like the external noise of life had quietened down, like at the beach in the evening after a hot summer's day. He made a good swing and hit as solid a 5 iron as I have ever seen him hit. A great tempo, a perfect sync of his arms and body into a controlled and balanced finish. It landed perfectly where he aimed and released up to 12 feet from the hole, almost as close as you could safely hit it to. He took a little time, soaking in the shot he had just hit. I complimented him on the shot and took off walking.

It is sometimes nice in a round to just walk on your own. Taking time to yourself to reflect on a shot as you transition to the next one or to simply let your thoughts drift off to think about life. Transitioning from one shot to the next relies on the same principles as it does when transitioning in life.

THE NOW

When we go from one shot to the next or we transition in life, like from work to home, it's important to process the transition correctly and to observe and reflect on what you experienced in your first space and what it means to you. And then transition into the next golf shot or next space in your life with a refreshed and renewed energy. An energy that carries the intentions required to get the outcome you're looking for. In golf, if you don't mindfully transition or detach, you may get stuck in the space and energy of the previous shot, or your thoughts drift to a place that then affects your state.

The Bible teaches to take your thoughts captive. That would support the notion that we do have control of our thoughts and it's our responsibility to control them and have them work for us and not against us. So, think about things that enhance a positive state. Think about people and events that bring life force energy. If you're led into a conversation that isn't uplifting, divert the conversation to one that is more positive.

We walked onto the green in our own time and went about our putting preparations as though we were playing on our own. Sometimes humans just need their own space and energy zones, be it at golf, work, home, or socially. We both had strong intentions of capitalising on our solid tee shots. The 11th green has very subtle breaks. My putt looked a little left to right, but I knew from experience that, if anything, it would go left. I aimed at the right edge and struck a beautiful putt that stayed on the line of the right edge. It rolled past the right edge by about a foot, an easy tap in at the optimum holing speed. Steve was very clear with his intentions; he said he was aiming at centre-cup, appearing confident in his conviction. It seemed as though he was certain this was going in. He went through his routine with an ease and certainty of achieving his desired outcome, and that's exactly what happened. His ball rolled purely into the centre of the hole, and he strolled up to retrieve it with calmness and knowing. A little fist pump to each other and simultaneous smiles suggested we were both in golf bliss.

I walked to the 12th tee, grateful to share this day and this bliss with a long-time friend. Great moments and success in life seem so much more meaningful when they are shared with people you love and appreciate.

Sage Advice on The Now

- The now is the isolation of time between the past and the future.
- Everything you do is in the now. What you have done is in the past and what you hope to do is in the future.
- You know you're in the now when you are free of doubt and fear and feel at peace.

The Now

The present moment is the only place where the fullness of life truly unfolds. To be aware and focused on the now is to experience the true magic of existence. In this space, where mind, body, and spirit are fully present, we can express our holistic best. Doubts, fears, and frictions vanish, replaced by complete presence and the permission to express our utmost potential.

Existing in the now offers a glimpse of eternity – a joy, love, and peace that surpasses all understanding. Have you ever hit a golf shot that felt thought-free and effortless, as if it happened outside of yourself and beyond the constraints of time? In that moment, all noise subsided, conscious thought disappeared, and watching the ball soar was a blissful experience. That's the power of the now.

In this place, all desires are detached. Intention remains, but without attachment to outcomes. Accessing the now has long been shrouded in mysticism, often perceived as requiring something external. But the now is accessible to all. It begins with focusing on one thing in the present moment, letting go of distractions, and detaching from outcomes. Your breath is the anchor to the now.

There are no absolutes from one moment to the next. However, one thing is certain – anxiety and doubt are both tied to beliefs in undesirable outcomes. Some people are medicated for anxiety, conditioned from an early age. Yet, an adult upgrade to one's belief system can dismantle old, detrimental beliefs and replace them with new, congruent ones that foster a calm disposition despite challenges. If you're going to expend energy predicting the future, envision a positive one.

Living in the now requires reconciling with the polarity of the first two of six core human needs: certainty and variety. Many people struggle to stay in the present due to the discomfort of uncertainty that may arise from challenging situations or not knowing an outcome. This is similar to the anxious feelings many golfers experience – whether it is an opening tee shot or a putt they feel they should make.

The key is to breathe and establish a routine that instils a sense of certainty and calm. Accept the variety and uncertainty of the upcoming shot. Understand that the shot holds no inherent meaning until you assign it one. It does not reflect your value and worth as a person unless you allow it to. Each shot is merely an opportunity to assess whether your practice is effective or if there is more to learn and grow.

The true existence in the now is where the mind, body, and spirit unite, allowing you to perform at your best. Embrace this moment, free from attachments and distractions, and let the present reveal the magic within you.

Sage Questions on The Now

1. Do you have an anchor, such as a specific breathing pattern, that helps you stay in the now? How does it work for you?

   _____
   _____
   _____
   _____

2. Are you aware you are fully present on the golf course? What signs or feelings indicate that you are in the now?
   _____
   _____
   _____
   _____

3. Is there a daily exercise you have or could have to practice being in the now?
   _____
   _____
   _____

A Model of The Now: Jack Nicklaus

The now and transition space are inexplicably linked and deeply intertwined. To transition well, you must be in the now, and to be in the now, you must transition well. It stands to reason then that Jack Nicklaus is again a great example of playing golf in the now. He was so clear about his strategy and intentions that his visualisations created a powerful connection to the present moment. The overflow was that he was so often in the now. Who could ever forget Jack Nicklaus winning the US Masters at 46 years of age? He shot 30 on the back nine to win the last of his six US Masters. As he recounted in many previous victories, his focus was on one shot at a time, staying in the now – calm, focused, and committed.

Jack's ability to immerse himself in the present moment, whether in a golf tournament or during his day-to-day life, was a testament to the power of the now. He was known for his disciplined approach to golf, meticulously planning each shot while remaining fully present in the moment of execution. This clarity of mind and presence allowed him to consistently perform at the highest level, even under the most intense pressure.

Nicklaus's legacy extended beyond his record-setting victories; it's also in how he mastered the mental game of golf. His ability to stay in the now was not just a technique but a way of being that permeated all aspects of his life. Whether on the golf course, in business, or with his family, Jack Nicklaus exemplified the power of living fully in the present, showing that true success is deeply rooted in the now.

CHAPTER 12
FOCUS

"Focus is the force that drives you towards your desired outcome; distraction is what draws you away."

Hole 12

The twelfth hole was a 517 metre par 5. The tees were forward about 10 metres, making it reachable with two strong shots. The tee shot was a little into the breeze. Standing in the middle of the tee, looking down the fairway, I said to Steve, "Imagine if there was just this tee, the green, and all lush fairway – no bunkers, no rough, no trees. It would be a little bland and boring. Courses are designed to challenge us, to draw out our creativity and skill. Great course designers effectively help create great golfers. Now, with that in mind, Steve, it's your honour after that impressive birdie. Pick your target where you want the ball to finish, pick a starting line that matches the shot required to finish where you want it. Be confident, be committed, and let it rip."

He smiled a reassuring smile and did just that. He ripped his best tee shot of the day – a straight ball that gently moved on the left-to-right breeze and finished dead centre of the fairway. Now it was time for me to smoke what I'm selling and do the same thing.

BEYOND THE FAIRWAYS TO FULFILMENT

Before playing, I like to do a short five to ten-minute meditation or breathing exercise. It works by bringing me into the present moment and my ideal state, and by serving as an anchor to refocus if I drift out of that state mid-round.

As I stood on the tee, I did a quick box breathing exercise – for four seconds each: breathe in, hold, exhale, hold again, and repeat. I looked down the fairway as I contrasted in my head the image of an open, lush, boring field with the reality that lay before me. I committed to the same line and shape as Steve. I walked into the ball with clear intentions, a strong but soft setup over the ball, one last look, and then let fly with an aggressive swing. It flew over by Steve's ball and finished about 25 metres past it. We strolled down the fairway talking about his upcoming holiday to Italy and France for Steve and his wife Sam's 30th wedding anniversary. As a young Christian couple when they got married, they successfully navigated raising four children – two their birth children and two very blessed adopted children. Both running successful businesses at different times and continuing to maintain their love for each other and their commitment to their faith. They are a wise and caring couple, who I have always admired and appreciated in my life. I was brimming with excitement hearing about their itinerary.

We reached Steve's ball and estimated the distance at 260 metres. We discussed his options. There were three bunkers to consider and one fairway bunker to navigate. He couldn't reach the green, so the decision was all about where best to play his third shot. The right fairway bunker needed to be avoided, sitting 40 metres short right of the green, while the other two bunkers were left greenside bunkers. It was visually a fairly tight shot. Steve decided hitting down the left side to avoid the bunker was the best option, aiming to leave about 70 metres for a full lob wedge to ensure he could stop it quickly. He needed to hit a shot about 190 metres, his 3-rescue club. It was a shot that needed as much commitment and aggression as any.

Often, when golfers take a conservative strategy, they accompany the strategy with a conservative swing, which can often result in a poorly struck shot. I reminded him to be committed and aggressive. He made a practice swing that looked like he was in his groove. He hit a nice shot in perfect position down the left centre. He was beaming like a kid in a candy shop.

I had 235 metres to the hole, about 215 metres to the front of a slightly elevated green. I assessed that I wanted to start the ball on the right edge of the left greenside bunker, let it fade a touch, and release up to the hole. I walked into the ball on autopilot, saying the 9s in my head, taking aim. There was one long nine in my head as I swung, and it was a peach of a shot. Just flush out of the middle, it looked as good in the air as it did at the finish. It just caught a bit of an upslope before the green and didn't release as much as I had anticipated. It finished about 35 feet short left of the pin.

My recent Mizuno club fitting was a great experience. Charlie, their fitter, did an excellent job, and I was super happy with the result. At the fit, we started with a 14-degree 3-wood that could go 240 metres. I asked if we could go with a 15-degree 3-wood that goes slightly higher and knocks the distance back to about 230 metres. My reasoning was for this very scenario – needing to flight and stop a 3-wood on a par 5. Thanks to Charlie and me working together, I was confident that I had the club to reach the front edge and finish up close to that hole.

I strongly believe in being fitted properly for all golf clubs, from driver to putter. I believe through technology and expertise, the leading companies do it best. And Mizuno is exceptional, building each individual club to an incredible standard. They literally weigh and match every single component of each individual club to the exact requirement of a player and continue that process for the entire set.

Steve had 73 metres to the pin – a fairly full lob wedge was required. In his mind, he thought he needed to hit it very solid to play the shot he wanted. He forced it a little and, as a result, pulled it about 15 feet left of the hole, but it was a good length. I had a 35-foot putt. The PGA Tour average is less than 10 percent from this range. I always have the intention of holing a putt this length unless there is a severe slope, but I'm respectful of the data from this range and certainly work hard on not being attached to the outcome or needing to make the putt. It was a slightly left-to-right breaking putt. I had the feel for it and struck a great putt that finished inches away on the right side. Two high-quality shots, a good long putt and a tap-in for a nice birdie 4.

Steve sized up his putt, which was slightly downhill and required a good touch. He erred on the conservative side and left it short right – a stress-free par – but I could see he really wanted to make a birdie 4 after his first two solid shots. Wanting and needing are often emotions people go to, but they are emotions that don't serve us well. Having intentions but not being attached or having any neediness is a far better way of living and offers far greater access to peak performances.

Sage Advice on Focus

- Focus moves your attention to the desired outcome.
- Focus in golf happens both at a conscious and subconscious level.
- Focus is like true north, a constant light that guides you despite distractions.

You're reading this book, so you can focus. Most people have a great capacity to focus when in an optimal state. It's not so much about improving focus as it is about not being easily distracted. The modern world is filled with electronic distractions. Marketing experts are vying for our attention, pulling us away from what's truly important: faith, family, and becoming the best version of ourselves. The same principle applies on the golf course. Good golf course architects create distractions to divert the golfer's focus from what they want to achieve to what they fear.

To avoid distractions and optimise focus, be very clear about your intentions and objectives. Once you are clear about the desired outcome, amplify your intentions and objectives by understanding why you want what you want. The 'why' acts as a beacon for your focus, a constant source of energy, and an anchor in turbulent times. Knowing that the reason is worth the payoff of the challenge helps maintain your focus.

Once focused, it is important to be aware of your holistic state – how you feel emotionally and physically. Maintaining your state is crucial for sustaining focus. Distractions come in various forms: physical, mental and spiritual. Some distractions stem from past experiences and indoctrinations from family, friends, and schooling. Spiritual distractions are also significant. As the Bible says, the thief (the devil) comes to steal, kill, and destroy – these are all very distracting actions. Therefore, it's important to guard against distractions by focusing on the right things.

On the golf course, having a good strategy and an understanding of the course is essential for maintaining focus. Some people prefer picking small targets, like leaves in trees or patches of grass. Others find small targets anxiety-inducing and prefer larger targets, like the whole tree or the middle of the fairway. Regardless, having a clear target is crucial for maintaining focus. Another common distraction on the golf course is asking poor questions. Questions like, "What if I hit it out of bounds?" or "What happens if I miss this putt?" only serve to increase anxiety. Instead, ask yourself better questions: "What would I like to happen here?" and "Where is the best place for me to hit the ball?" or "What's the best shot to achieve my desired outcome?" Determine your target, your starting line, and your shot shape.

Asking quality questions clarifies your intentions. Where there is intention, attention follows. And where attention goes, energy flows, enhancing and maintaining focus. Intentions are like a magnetic force, drawing your focus towards the desired outcome. In the end, focus is not just about directing your attention but also about managing distractions. By setting clear objectives, maintaining your holistic state, guarding against various forms of distractions, and asking quality questions, you can achieve a heightened and sustained level of focus. This practice not only improves your golf game but also enriches your life, allowing you to pursue and achieve your best self.

Sage Questions on Focus

1. How can you focus better in your day-to-day activities? Do you have habitual distractions?

    _____
    _____
    _____
    _____

2. What specific processes or mental anchors do you use on the golf course to maintain strong focus throughout your round?

    _____
    _____
    _____
    _____

3. What are the signs that indicate you are in a highly focused state, and how can you recognise and replicate this state more consistently?

    _____
    _____
    _____
    _____

Models of Focus: Ben Hogan, Jack Nicklaus and Tiger Woods

When you hear the word 'focus' in golf, three names are always at the forefront: Ben Hogan, Jack Nicklaus and Tiger Woods. These three golfers were very intentional about what they wanted to achieve in their careers, in each tournament, and in each practice session. Nicklaus was meticulous with his course strategy and visualisation of each shot to maintain supreme focus. Woods used meditation techniques along with visualisation sessions to boost his focus superpower. His mental and physical routine was also crucial to his deep focus and commitment to each shot. Hogan's meticulous attention to detail in his golf swing, innovative thinking and relentless practice culminated in a man with pure focus. The love of the game, the commitment to continuous improvement, and the deep satisfaction in mastering their craft were fundamental to their exceptional focus and success.

CHAPTER 13
RESILIENCE

"Resilience is the ability to stand back up when life knocks you down."

Hole 13

We stood on the thirteenth tee a 405 metre par 4, looking down the fairway formulating a strategy. Steve expressed his disappointment in not making his birdie putt on the last hole. "It would have been nice to make birdie there and have some breathing space," Steve said. I understood that he was saying "I'm likely to make some mistakes at some stage, so if I can get some birdies in the bank, then that will soften the blow of a bogey later on. I replied and said "If you're clear with your intentions, visualise the shot, focus and commit fully to each shot you won't need to protect your score, you will improve it. What's more, trust that you have the resilience and capacity to respond well to any challenges you may face in the remaining holes and that in itself will give you confidence that will help you to play well.

In the past year, I had some lessons from a friend of mine, Brett Lebroque. I've known Brett a long time, and he always helps me whenever I reach out to him, and not just for golf. He once commented that he wished he had shown me these changes years ago, but I felt I simply wasn't ready. Many times golf had knocked me down metaphorically, and I thought, *I'm done, I can't get up.* But fortunately, I did, and I got to reap the rewards of building resilience. Now, nothing that happens to me when playing golf will ever knock me to a point of wanting to quit. The challenges and setbacks that almost broke my resilience were a beautiful test that ultimately made me a better player and a more resilient person. So, with Brett's great wisdom and help, I built a strong and consistent golf swing, one I trust in.

It was my honour this time, and the combination of the right-to-left wind and the right-to-left sloping fairway made for a green light for hitting an aggressive drive.

Visualising the shot, having a clear target shot shape and starting line are paramount. That, coupled with a sound routine and solid swing fundamentals make for a consistent golfer. When you think about it, hitting a good golf shot is complex; however, golf is best played with simple and efficient processes; it is best played with feel rather than thought.

I often choose small targets, especially off the tee, like a branch of a tree, a pole, or part of a cloud – it's a personal preference. For some golfers, something a little bigger may be more beneficial – perhaps a house, a tree or a whole cloud. Whatever the case, know what works for you and stick to it.

Then enter the shot, as Bruce Lee would say, "Be like water, my friend," and without thought I wondered how Bruce would have fared as a golfer? He was the greatest martial artist of his time, but I think golf would have certainly challenged him. My starting line was the edge of a grey-rendered double-story house, a fairly straight shot, that would drift back on the wind.

I like playing with some wind as I feel it makes shaping the shot easier. And I think shaping a shot allows me to feel it easier than I could compared to a straight shot.

When I first started playing golf in the mid-80s, we had persimmon woods; metal drivers were not heard of, and the balls were softer and would stay on the clubface longer, making it easier to shape the ball. That style definitely suited my game a lot more. The modern-day ball and modern-day clubs are designed for a harder and faster collision between the clubface and the ball, making it easier to hit it straight and harder to shape it. As for left-to-right or right-to-left wind preference, I prefer a right-to-left wind, but I'm certainly comfortable with left-to-right. After all, what you need to do with any wind is pick a starting line, hit your natural shot shape, and work with the wind to move back to your target. It's best to use the wind where you can, rather than fight it.

So, I felt extremely confident with this shot and hit it accordingly. My drive started at the edge of the house, drifted a little on the breeze, followed the slope of the fairway, and finished centre left of the fairway. Steve stood on the tee and said, "Right, I'll follow that shot." This was the most peaceful and confident I had ever seen him play. He teed it up in the centre of the tee markers, aimed down the right side, and made another free-flowing swing. It followed my line and settled about 20 metres behind me. As we walked off the tee, I said to him that he looked relaxed in himself and his swing. He said the myofascial release work we did had wound his body clock back 15 years. He said, "I feel so much freer everywhere. You know, just reframing how I see the golf course as a guide and not an opponent, as a guide that wants me to play well, has given me a peace I have never had before." I was a little surprised at the impact of such a simple reframe. When I related my little daydreaming experience on the first tee, I didn't think it would have such a profound impact.

I smiled at him and said, "Well, make sure you make the myofascial release a regular part of your golf routine and use this new perspective of the golf course a part of the mental framework in which you play your golf." Adding, "Our thoughts and our perspectives are our responsibility."

We arrived at Steve's ball. The 13th green was an elevated two-tiered green. The flag was on the top tier, left of centre. The left side of the green was guarded by a big greenside bunker. A bunker short right, that doesn't really come into play with a back-left pin position, was merely a potential visual distraction. The ideal leave for any back pin position was a straight uphill putt from the centre of the green. Short right of the pin gave a straight uphill putt, but if you were too short it would come back down leaving a long up-tier putt. A pin-high shot would leave a right-to-left putt. We discussed all the variables. Sometimes too many options lead to confusion; but usually you have an intuitive first choice if you're tuned into your instinct. Steve had just over 100 metres to the front of the green, but with the two-tiered green, the distance to the pin was 134 metres. Steve felt that a solidly struck 8-iron should land around the centre of the green and release forward a bit. He was confident he had the right club to finish on the top level, which was the key to this shot.

I remembered a story of Greg Norman. He was undoubtedly a great player, but in my opinion, he underachieved in never winning a US Major. I think his ego tried desperately to protect his insecurities, and he paid a massive price for not having the awareness or courage to face his insecurities. He was confronted with a pivotal shot in a US Open to a double-tiered green. He wanted to hit a 5-iron, but his caddy, Steve Williams, the most successful caddy in history, said, "It's a 4-iron; you need a 4-iron to get it on the top tier." Norman, as was often the case, let his ego call the shots. He took the 5-iron, but it didn't reach the top tier, leaving him a long up-tier putt – he three-putted and lost the tournament by a shot.

Fortunately, Steve doesn't have a disempowering ego and makes what I agree to be the best choice. He said, "I'll aim at the right side of the green, allow for the wind to move it a little to the left, but still get it to finish right of the flag." A very good strategy.

He made a practice swing, just clipping the grass nicely. Committed to his shot, he walked in, his alignment looked perfect, he made a good, synchronised swing and hit the ball nicely off the tight Santa Ana Couch fairway. Just as he had spoken, it landed in the centre of the green, released up the green, and finished around pin high, 25 feet from the hole.

I had 113 metres to a slightly elevated green. It was not quite a full wedge.

I play these shots with a shorter but more aggressive swing, so they come out a little lower, take a solid first bounce but stop quickly. This type of hole is pivotal for momentum. If you play one shot at a time in the present moment, it is a very easy hole. But if you start pushing for birdies and focusing on the future and the non-controllable, then you open the door to disaster.

I was committed to a slightly conservative target with an aggressive swing planning for a 15-foot pin-high putt. I looked around at the sky, the clouds and the ground beneath me to get back to the now. I made a practice swing and I knew I was in the now – just moving moment to moment. I stood behind the ball in my zone one, the assessment and thinking zone. I took a deep breath, tugged my shirt over my left shoulder, stepped forward into the hitting zone, and just let my subconscious do its job. The whole process seemed effortless and serene. I took aim, my body wiggled here and there, then before I knew it, the ball was humming in the air. A crisp strike with a good rate of spin, and it came to rest very close to my 15-foot target to right of the hole.

It's sometimes frustrating that we pick the correct strategic target, which is mostly a little conservative, then have a slight regret that we didn't just aim at the flag. But it's in making the correct and often conservative target choice that we free ourselves of anxieties that a risky target would create. This allows us access to a free-flowing swing and shot as we fully trust our conservative choice. I assure you that intelligent strategic targets, in the long run, will allow you to play far more consistent golf than playing on ego and emotions.

The strategy of Decade Golf is used by the best players in the world because it's the best way to play consistent golf.

Steve had 25 – 30 feet slightly downhill with some right to left. I always advocate that on big-breaking putts, you must err on the high side of the hole. Die the big-breaking putts into the hole. So, Steve had been well drilled over the years to err high. He looked at this putt and visualised the line and speed at which it would roll. He had a couple of practice strokes that looked perfect for the putt he was about to hit. He stood over the putt and stroked it with a similar tempo. It started three feet right of the hole and seemed like it was in slow motion. It slowly but steadily continued to roll and break towards the hole. We both looked intently as it looked a great chance of going in – it was slowing down and breaking. Steve started raising his putter in a triumphant victory salute. The putt slid by the right lip, grabbing a small but insufficient part of the hole and finished inches past. There was a cry of, "Oh ah, so close!" from Steve. I grinned and said, "Great putt, I thought you had holed it."

I had a 15-foot pin-high putt that had about two feet of break. This putt was also going to be just dying in. I had a couple of practice strokes; I knew I was taking a conservative line. This putt was struck sweetly out of the middle of the putter; it tracked on a beautiful line but pulled up three inches short, right on target. This hole played quite easily, and we both played it in a manner that made it look and feel like a straightforward hole.

For all the technicalities spoken of putting, hitting out of the sweet spot of the putter is one of the most important aspects. I've worked hard in recent times with the EyeLine sweet spot putting aid and have improved the consistency with which I strike the putt.

Good strategies will quite often leave you with the feeling that the hole played easily, and that's a stress-free way to play and enjoy golf. Visualise the shot you want, feel it, and execute it.

Sage Advice on Resilience

- Resilience shows you where you are strong and where you can get stronger.
- Resilience is necessary for growth.
- Resilience is a great ingredient in confidence.

Resilience

Resilience is the ability to bounce back from setbacks or adversity. Life is beautiful; it's a great gift, but it certainly comes with challenging times, and these challenging times will test and build your resilience.

Your resilience show cases a lot of your identity; resilience will display your physical, mental and emotional fortitude and strength. Challenging times are also an opportunity to build and strengthen your resilience.

Resilience challenges your mindset toolkit. It may challenge you to ask these questions: Is this challenge personal? Is this happening to me because there is something inherently wrong with me? It is never personal. Tough times and challenges do not discriminate; everyone will face them at some stage. If you find yourself asking, "Why is this happening to me?", ask it from the perspective of finding the gift in the challenge, not from a "poor me" vantage point.

Golfers hit shots and sometimes may get what is judged as an unlucky bounce. They lament, "Why am I always so unlucky?" They soon forget all the fortunate bounces they had previously received. They perceive the bad luck as a personal attack and, in so doing, forfeit the opportunity to build their resilience muscles.

Good luck and bad luck are man-made mechanisms, used to rationalise and make sense of events. The reality is, good and bad are perceptions of reality, not necessarily the truth. Getting fixated on judging a situation only restricts you from taking the necessary action to overcome the challenge and get you back on track and focused on your desired outcomes.

When a situation challenges your resilience, it's a great opportunity to address all the facets of your identity. What character traits, skills and strengths can you put to use to get your desired outcome? What facets of your identity can you prune and replace to better overcome this challenge and grow beyond it?

Given that through many life cycles and patterns, disruption follows intention, it is inevitable that as you start out in pursuit of a goal or objective, you will be challenged or knocked off course. Your resilience will be tested physically, mentally and/or spiritually. You will need resilience to bounce back and realign yourself to your intentions and desired outcomes.

Humans by nature like to avoid pain and prefer to seek pleasure. So, it's difficult to see the necessity in challenges. If a caterpillar didn't use its resilience and struggle through the cocoon, it would never become the butterfly. If athletes and people wanting to get stronger didn't struggle and fail to lift heavy weights, they wouldn't get stronger.

Laws of nature suggest that there must often be struggle before there is success. No humans would be born if it wasn't for the fortitude of women to show great resilience and give birth. Children attempt to stand up many times, only to fall down many times before their resilience is rewarded.

Resilience is an important component in the success of a human. Many people have endured setbacks that built their resilience, and they go on to become great people. Resilience is fundamental to greatness.

Golf is an extremely challenging game and all golfers experience disappointment. But the golfers who fulfil their potential use the disappointments and setbacks that golf dishes out to their advantage. They use the setbacks to build their resilience muscles.

Resilient people bounce back better and stronger than they were before the setback. They see the gift in the challenge. Resilient people don't take setbacks and disappointments personally, they know they are temporary and that they do not define them. Their value and worth cannot be diminished through adversity but it can aid them to become a better, more valuable human being.

Resilience, although built through the commitment to persevere in challenging times, is ultimately the by-product of choice. You don't necessarily get to choose all your life or golf challenges, but you do get to choose the level of resilience you will use to succeed despite these challenges.

RESILIENCE

Challenges that test your resilience are an opportunity to take inventory of your physical, mental and spiritual capacities and assess where you can strengthen them and best prepare for the next time you will require your resilience muscles.

Sage Questions on Resilience

1. What has been a life challenge that has gone on to be a gift in building your resilience?

    _____
    _____
    _____
    _____

2. How could you better build your resilience on the golf course, that would ultimately see you play more consistently and enjoy your golf more often?

    _____
    _____
    _____
    _____

3. How could you better equip yourself holistically so you are more resilient for any life challenges that you will inevitably face?

    _____
    _____
    _____
    _____

Models of Resilience: Ben Hogan and Lee Trevino

Two golfers who could have had their careers shortened were Ben Hogan and Lee Trevino. Hogan had a bad car accident in 1949 and nearly died. He spent

59 days in the hospital, and with great resilience, he was back practicing months later and won the PGA Championship 11 months after his accident. Lee Trevino was struck by lightning in the 1975 Western Open; he was knocked unconscious and suffered bad burns. His determination and resilience had him back playing golf six weeks after the near-death experience. Both Hogan and Trevino expressed their resilience in their capacity to practice long and hard. They were relentless in their work ethics and resilient in their ability to compete at the highest level for many years. Lesser men may never have returned to professional golf given the severity, but their love of the game and a desire to live a purposeful life drove both men's resilience.

CHAPTER 14
SIX CORE NEEDS

"Needs trump values. While values guide us, core needs drive our behaviour and shape our lives."

Hole 14

The fourteenth hole was a 364 metre par 4 with fairway bunkers left off the tee, and an elevated green that runs unusually steep from front to back that is guarded by deep bunkers short and right of the green, long and right of the green, and left centre of the green. It's a challenging green but a smart design. It requires an approach with great accuracy, distance control, and a good strategy. But for now, it's all about the tee shot. Often, smart architects take into consideration the mental focus required for certain holes. I feel like 13 and 14 are fairly easy holes if you play them correctly, but a lapse in concentration could bring your whole round undone.

There was a left-to-right breeze off the tee. The right side of the fairway is wide and forgiving, but it runs off into the right rough and makes for a tougher approach shot than the left side of the fairway.

I chose a red-bricked cart path as my starting line down the left side of the fairway. I visualised that the breeze would move it off that line into the middle of the fairway. I had a good drink of water and a chicken, avocado and salad wrap when walking to the tee. I was very mindful to stay hydrated and well-fuelled when playing golf. I felt the snack gave me a little boost for the home stretch. I took aim at the cart path and swung with a well-sequenced swing that produced a perfectly flighted shot at the path with a slightly lower flight than usual. It ran to the centre of the fairway into a perfect position.

Steve was still munching on an apple. I said, "Just swallow before you start your routine." He smirked like a kid in trouble, but he knew what I was implying: don't rush, stay in your optimal state. He finished his mouthful of apple and said just a little right of that cart path was good for him. He went through his routine and cracked one just on the left edge of the cart path. He pulled it a fraction; it came out a little lower but with a bit of a run on it, which left a very good angle into the green.

Steve had 124 metres to the pin, a left-to-right breeze, and a green sloping hard front to back. It was best to be past this pin, but you needed to land it well short to even achieve that. Steve planned on flying a high wedge about 112 metres, about a third of the way on the green, and letting it release. The pin was about two-thirds of the way down the green on the right side, but you didn't want to miss it on that side. Steve aimed for a spot two metres left of the pin, knowing it would feed left but be safe. It was a narrow landing area. I could see and hear that he was committed to this smart strategy. He had a couple of smooth practice swings, settled over the ball, looked at his target, then back to the ball, and made a very compact swing. It came out a little lower due to the compact compression, but it had a good amount of spin. Although it released fairly hard as expected, you could tell it was trying to grip. It came to rest about 18 feet long and left of the hole, leaving an ideal uphill putt. I had 109 metres to the pin and anticipated that if I flew my sand wedge about 102 metres, the ball should release about seven metres and be close. I flew it about 105 metres with a crisp strike, but it finished about 15 feet past the pin.

Steve sized up his putt; it was uphill, right-to-left with what looked like about a foot of break. He hit it slightly higher and missed on the high side by half a foot for an easy tap-in par. I had about 15 feet. It looked straight up the hill. I went through my routine and felt comfortable and confident. I settled over the putt, but it felt like it could go a touch left. I backed off the putt and took another look – it still looked fairly straight. OK, I had to trust it. I went through my routine again and struck a nice putt out of the middle of the putter. It looked on-line until about a metre out, then fell left of the hole for an easy par. After making a few early birdies, a couple of pars could weirdly feel like you were losing momentum. But the key was to stay in the now, feel the breeze, look at your surroundings, sense the ground beneath your feet, and breathe. And take a mindful drink of water, which we both did.

Sage Advice on Six Core Needs

- These needs will be met either resourcefully or unresourcefully.
- Your behaviour is an attempt to meet one or more of these needs.
- Needs trump values.

The six core needs provide a framework to understand human behaviour and motivation, which can be relevant to developing a strong golf mindset. These needs explain why we act the way we do and how they shape our behaviour on the golf course. Once you understand the six core needs, you can start to understand human behaviour. Behaviour can be connected to being an attempt to meet one or more of these needs. What adds more clarity to people's behaviour is that needs trump values.

Certainty/Comfort

This need is about safety, comfort and control. For golfers, certainty is established through consistent practice routines, using the same equipment, playing with the same people at the same time, and having a playing and scoring comfort zone. These people do well with consistency, such as pre-game and pre-shot routines. It helps build confidence and reduces the anxiety of uncertainty. These golfers can really struggle when circumstances and situations suddenly change. By understanding the core needs and their impact on behaviour, you can simply take a breath, articulate to yourself that the manifested feelings of uncertainty are just feelings. They are the results of conditioned thoughts. If you breathe and remain calm, this situation can be an opportunity to stretch, grow and learn.

Uncertainty/Variety

Golf inherently involves a lot of uncertainty and variety, from changing weather conditions to different course layouts and unpredictable outcomes of each shot. Embracing this need helps golfers stay adaptable, engaged and open to new experiences. Balancing certainty and variety is crucial; too much certainty leads to boredom, while too much variety can be unsettling.

Significance

Many golfers seek recognition, whether it's winning tournaments, achieving personal bests, or gaining respect from other players. This need can motivate them to strive to perform at their best and push their limits. However, if the need for significance becomes too dominant, it can lead to ego-driven behaviour and excessive pressure to perform, which may negatively impact the enjoyment and performance.

Love and Connection

Golfers often form strong bonds with their playing partners and the golfing community. This need for meaningful relationships and connectedness motivates players to continue participating in the sport. However, prioritising connection over significance might mean choosing to play with friends who are less skilled rather than with better players who could help improve their game.

Growth

The continuous pursuit of personal mastery is a key motivator in golf. Golfers are always striving to improve their skills, lower their scores, and master the mental aspects of the game. This need drives constant learning and improvement, making it a fundamental part of a golfer's journey.

Contribution

Golfers often feel a need to give back, whether through mentoring younger players, participating in charity tournaments, or contributing to their club's teams and community. This need to add value and make a difference can enhance a golfer's sense of purpose and fulfilment in the sport.

There are four key insights about how these needs operate in our lives that must be understood to make this model really work:

i. These six needs will inevitably be fulfilled, one way or another. If you don't have an intentional approach to meet your needs in a constructive way, you may eventually turn to behaviors that are not aligned to your values to meet those needs.

ii. Don't just stop – swap. Since needs are always active, trying to eliminate a behavior without replacement is unlikely to work. To shift any unhelpful behavior, you need to substitute it with an empowering behavior that serves the same purpose. Otherwise, you may end up adopting a similarly disempowering behavior, to fulfill the underlying need.

iii. Needs take priority over values. Needs demand fulfilment, sometimes even at the expense of what matters most to you. This is often why people may act in ways that go against their values. It explains why someone who values honesty might lie, or why someone who values health might smoke. Unmet needs can drive actions that conflict with one's core beliefs.

iv. Every negative behavior has a positive intention behind it. It's essential to remember that people are not defined by their actions alone. Often, they engage in harmful behavior because of unmet needs, not because they are inherently bad. Instead of fighting against these needs, the goal is to find fulfilling and value-aligned ways to meet them.

Sage Questions on Six Core Needs

1. What are three things that are important to you in life? How do these relate to your core needs in golf and life?

   _____
   _____
   _____
   _____

2. How could you use the core needs as superpowers to get more from life that you desire?

   _____
   _____
   _____
   _____

3. What specific need do you recognise as most dominant in your life and golf? How could you ensure that this need is met resourcefully rather than unresourcefully?

   _____
   _____
   _____
   _____

A Model of Six Core Needs: Gary Player

The great South African golfer Gary Player is a great example of the resourceful application of the six core needs in both golf and life. His certainty came from his incredible work ethic both on the golf range and in the gym, which gave him great confidence in his game. His variety was sourced through his busy international schedule. He was known as the International Ambassador of Golf. Beyond golf, he enjoyed a variety of activities, including reading, golf course design, and a strong interest in horses.

His significance came from winning 165 tournaments worldwide and nine major championships, and achieving the career Grand Slam, bringing him recognition and respect. He was inducted into the World Golf Hall of Fame and received numerous accolades. His love and connection were built through strong relationships with fans, fellow golfers, and the golfing community. His sportsmanship and engaging personality helped him connect with people worldwide. His family played a central role in his life, and he has often spoken about the importance of family and close relationships. His philanthropic work also demonstrates a deep connection to and care for others.

His growth was evident in his dedication to continuously working on improving his game, adapting to changes in the sport, and maintaining his physical fitness, even as he aged. His drive for self-improvement was evident throughout his career. He pursued various interests that stretched him as a person and expanded his influence beyond playing golf, including course design, authorship, and motivational speaking, reflecting commitment to personal and professional growth.

His contributions to the sport, his pioneering role in international golf, and his commitment to fitness and health have left a lasting legacy, making him a significant figure in sports history and a great contributor.

CHAPTER 15
PEAK STATE

"Peak states empower you to reach the summits of your dreams."

Hole 15

As we walked to the fifteenth hole, for a 315-metre par 4, I said to Steve, "You're playing great." He replied, "Yes, but I'm starting to think about my score a little. What happens if I have a double bogey or a couple of bogeys like I have done in the past when playing well? I feel like I could ruin a great round."

I responded, "The quality of our questions can often determine the quality of our experiences and our lives. You could ask yourself, "What if I have some bogeys?" But may I suggest asking a better-quality questions such as, "What if all the great mindset work we've done together and all the quality practice we've put in, is about to pay off? What if I keep going through my routine, if I keep trusting myself, if I don't need or want anything from this round? What if I keep playing the game I'm playing and maintain the same state? What do you think may happen?" He smiled and said, "I'll probably keep enjoying this great round and have a great score."

I explained to him that his negative thinking was based on his past. Sure, he had finished off rounds in less than desirable ways. It's those negative memories that have some certainty about them. There is evidence that he had finished poorly in the past – irrefutable proof – but it requires faith to believe in a positive outcome. Steve was meeting the need for certainty, but in an unresourceful way. A more resourceful way to meet the need for certainty is through a sound routine. Don't stop a behaviour; swap it. Stop asking poor questions and self-sabotaging your rounds with a reliable pre-shot routine. A consistent routine brings certainty, comfort, and confidence – a resourceful way to meet a common need on the golf course.

The 15th hole was a great little challenge. At 315 metres, it was reachable for long hitters with the wind, and usually only a wedge-type of shot into the wind. The hole was playing into the breeze for us, which could in some ways, make the approach shot easier. There were a total of nine bunkers on the hole, as if the course designer was attempting to distract the golfer from its simplicity. The pin was on a small back tier, so being into the wind was a great help. The driver towards the left greenside bunkers was the play for me. You can't reach them, and it's safer than flirting with the five right-side bunkers. I planned to hit a very small fade. Hitting into the wind always added to the shape of a shot, so a two-metre fade would move 8 - 10 metres. I took aim at the right-hand edge of the left greenside bunker and smoked a beautiful little fade to the safety of the middle of the fairway.

Steve hit the ball fairly straight. If he really freewheeled, I think his best shots had a very slight draw to them. He aimed at the middle of the green, banking on a small draw. His practice swings and routine looked very free flowing. He took his setup, a loose waggle looking at his target, then hit another solid drive. This was the most focused and confident I had ever seen Steve play. The whole day had been played in a peak state with good, positive vibes. I walked off while he went to his bag. I liked taking little timeouts to myself, just taking in the surroundings, and having a good drink of water. Hydration and nutrition are very important in sport, especially in golf, given the duration of a round.

I stood near the side of Steve's ball, having a good look at the green and the shot that we were both faced with. Steve had a better angle in than me. He had

84 metres, which was a solid gap wedge for him into a slight breeze. This shot required very good distance control. It was not a pin to go straight at, so Steve aimed a couple of metres to the right, which was a good play. He planned on hitting it high so it would stop quickly on the small back tier. Again, his practice swings looked smooth and in sync. He took aim, had a little waggle, and hit a crisp shot. It came out a little lower than he hoped. He pleaded with it to get down; it landed just short of the hole but took a decent first bounce and finished at about 20 feet.

I had 70 metres, which I'd call a 9 o'clock lob wedge swing – a swing that feels more or less like a half swing. It's one of my favourite distances, and a distance Steve and I had recently been practicing. Often players have a couple of distances they prefer, and this is mine. It's a half swing back and strong pivot through with my 58-degree wedge, and it stops quickly. Usually, a golf green slopes predominantly from back to front. That being the case, it's often sound advice to hit high wedge shots to front hole locations, and lower shots to back hole locations to reduce the amount of backspin. But this pin was on a small top tier, which required a high shot that would stop quickly.

I decided I wanted to fly the shot 69 metres, let it take a bounce, and allow for a little backspin. I took a practice swing and with absolute trust and confidence walked into the shot. Silently whispering 9s in my head to keep my mind quiet and allowing my subconscious to do its job, I took aim, three feet right of the hole. My eyes traced back to the ball, and my pivot started back. It was a well-synchronised swing, crisp contact, and a perfectly balanced finish. The ball was heading exactly where I intended – a straight flight with a hint of draw off a slightly ball-above-feet lie that creates a draw-bias shot for a right-hander. It just missed the pin on the right-hand side, took two bounces, and spun back to a metre past the hole.

As Steve and I walked towards the green, Steve asked me what I thought was the best way to practice the wedge game. I think, given the great technology that we have nowadays, the likes of TrackMan sessions are a great starting place. Doing sessions around two to three swing lengths for your three to four wedges works well. Three swing lengths with three wedges provide nine different flighted shots for starters. Sometimes the distances may overlap, like a half pitching wedge may go as far as a full lob wedge or sand iron, but the flights and spins will be different. Working on carry distances is a good way to begin, but you also want to hit shots to land short or long of the target, depending on how receptive the green is. Launch angles can be helpful for getting consistent spin rates and knowing your optimal impact alignments.

Dropping a couple of extra balls in practice rounds and pitching to different distances under course conditions is also beneficial. Simulate pressure shots to understand your direction bias. Be mindful to do it from the edges of the fairway, replace your divots and especially fix your pitch marks.

Now, on the 15th green, we marked and cleaned our ball. If you were to roll golf balls off a stimpmeter, which is used to measure the speed of a green, you would see that the balls that are clean will roll out further than the balls that are unclean. It's always wise to mark and clean your ball unless it's inches away.

Steve sized his 20-footer up with intense focus. The discussion on the tee had empowered Steve to re-focus and maintain the great state he had been playing in. It had left-to-right break that required matching the speed to the correct line He sent it on its way, on what looked like a good speed and line. He was staring it down intently when it just missed on the high side. He fell to his knees in disbelief and mock despair. Nonetheless, an easy tap-in 4.

As a mindset coach, I could see that Steve was now starting to become attached to the outcome of his shots. When people start talking to the ball (which, I'm pretty sure don't have ears) and getting animated in their reactions to shots, it's a sign of attachment to the outcome, which will reduce the flow required for peak performance. My one metre putt was fairly routine – slightly uphill and straight. I had practiced this range quite a lot. I knew these were the putts you wanted to make no matter what pressure you were under. I went through my diligent routine. Aligning my eyes first, then my putter, then building my stance around that one last look at the hole. When I was settled and as soon as my eyes turned back to the ball, I started my stroke. My head remained steady until the ball went in the hole. Another easy birdie. Solid routines and quality practice sessions go a long way to meeting the need for certainty.

Sage Advice on Peak State

- An optimal state is a necessity for peak performances and your best life.
- A peak flow state is one where your attention is solely on the task at hand, where there is an inner calm that allows your mind and body to work in harmony.
- Intention, self-talk and physiology are three components that most influence our state.

Peak State

Your state is influenced by your thoughts, intentions, physiology, how your body is coping or responding to its environment, the language you are using, and your subjective interpretation of what you are experiencing.

The greater your awareness by way of both subjective and objective observation of what you are experiencing and the higher your emotional intelligence, the greater your chances of being in your optimal state.

The clearer you are about the outcomes you want, who you need to be to get those outcomes, and the greater the significance of why you want those outcomes – coupled with congruent thoughts, emotions, and actions – the greater your chance of being in and maintaining an optimal state.

Often, in the lead-up before people go on holidays, they get a lot done. They are excited and in a good state about the upcoming holiday. They are super focused on what they need to get done. They have a good 'why' as to why they want to get it done, so they can focus on their holiday and not the things they didn't get done. And as a result, they accomplish their tasks and enjoy their vacation.

Often, an optimal state is mystical and elusive – you may have sometimes experienced great states and been super productive or achieved outstanding results, but most times people get there by chance rather than by design. Having clear intentions is the starting point. It seems so obvious, but often people get caught up putting the cart before the horse and not starting where they ought to.

Intentions signal to the brain the outcome you desire. These signals then filter to our heart as emotions and feelings, and from your heart, you experience the manifestation in your hands as empowering and productive – or as disempowering and procrastination or stuck.

Rituals provide a framework and anchors in which you can purposefully and consistently access a desired state. Meditations, breathing exercises, and self-hypnosis are mechanisms that can help enter and maintain peak flow states. Often, these rituals will have an expiry date and will need to be updated and replaced. These rituals may include the clothes you wear, the perfume you wear, the music you listen to, a breathing exercise, or meditation, but they will no doubt have a season before you seek to update them. The magic is not in the rituals; they are just the entry point. The magic is in the state. You are constantly living your life in a state – live in a chosen state that gives you access to the outcomes you desire.

Sage Questions on Peak State

1. What intentional thoughts, emotions, or actions help you reach your peak state on the course?

_____
_____
_____
_____

2. What rituals or processes do you currently use to access a peak flow state in your activities or pursuits? How do these practices contribute to your performance and experience?

_____
_____
_____
_____

3. When disruptions arise, what helps you return to or maintain your peak state, and how do you keep it sustainable over a round?

_____
_____
_____
_____

Models of Peak State: Ben Hogan and Jack Nicklaus

It's not a coincidence that two of the absolute greats of the game – Jack Nicklaus and Ben Hogan were unflappable due to their state control. It was often the case that the higher the pressure, the better they performed. Both men rarely showed an emotion outside of their usual, very calm demeanour. They were both meticulous in their course management and strategies. They both practiced long and hard, had great self-belief in their abilities, and were both very resilient.

Winning a major certainly requires incredible state control. Nicklaus won his first U.S. Open major in a playoff in 1963, and 23 years later. Then, in 1986, through a peak performance state, he took out his legendary 18th major with his U.S. Masters win. Another legendary story of Jack's peak state under pressure came in the 1972 U.S. Open at Pebble Beach. During the final round, Nicklaus faced challenging conditions with high winds. On the 17th hole, a par 3 with the ocean on the left, Nicklaus hit a remarkable 1-iron shot that hit the flagstick and settled a few inches from the hole. Despite the difficult conditions, his focus and composure enabled him to execute the shot perfectly. Nicklaus won the tournament, solidifying his reputation as a clutch performer under pressure.

Hogan's unflappable peak state performance in his one and only British Open appearance and victory certainly solidified his legendary status. Known to the Brits as the 'Wee Ice Man' due to his demeanour, Hogan wowed the crowd with incredible skill and focus in what were very foreign conditions. And again, Hogan's legendary shot on the 72nd hole just 16 months after a near-fatal car accident – faced a gruelling 36-hole final day. On the 72nd hole, needing a par to force a playoff, Hogan hit a legendary 1-iron shot to the green under immense pressure. Despite his physical pain and fatigue, his focus and determination allowed him to execute the shot flawlessly. Hogan made the par, forced a playoff, and won the U.S. Open the next day, solidifying his comeback and mental toughness.

CHAPTER 16
CONFIDENCE

"The by-product of faithfully and honestly confiding in yourself daily."

Hole 16

We stood on the sixteenth hole and both took a moment to take in the surrounds and the day itself. We were both playing our best golf, enjoying the fantastic weather and a beautifully presented golf course. All these factors combined to have us in an optimal state for a great performance. Everything about our day had been state-enhancing, which led us to playing with great confidence.

We looked down the fairway of this 523m par 5 with an island-type green, guarded in front and left by a water hazard, and bunkers greenside right. It takes a very big hitter to reach the green in two. So, it was about finding the fairway off the tee, putting your second shot in a position that made for the easiest third shot, which being down breeze would only be a wedge shot. There was a bunker on the right and one on the left off the tee, but downwind I was confident I could get past them, even if I hit it at them. I aimed right down the middle, teed my ball a little higher so that I could hit it a bit higher than my standard drive and let the wind help gain a few extra metres. In the distance was a grey double-story house that was my target. I like downwind shots as I feel the ball goes straighter. I felt safe and at peace, making sure I embodied the advice I just gave Steve. I was in the now, a smile on my face, and just enjoying each moment.

Over the ball, I don't remember thinking anything, just feeling at peace. The whole swing felt like it happened on its own until I hit the ball and was coming to a balanced finish. The ball took off straight at the grey double-story house with a nice high flight. It flew past the line of the bunkers and bounded over a rise in the fairway and down the hill on the other side of the rise, in perfect position.

Steve made a smart decision to hit his 3-wood. He figured the bunkers were in play for him, so if he aimed down the right centre of the fairway, and if it had a touch of draw like his good ones did, he would be in a great position. He appeared focused on the shot at hand. He went through a good routine, with a smooth practice swing and no hesitation. He aimed exactly where he intended and hit a really solid 3-wood. It started down the right of centre, drew a couple of metres, and came to rest just short of the bunker line but in the middle of the fairway.

Steve's second shot needed to be about 200 metres, 220 maximum. He decided his rescue would be ideal for length and would leave him about 100 metres for his third shot. It was a smart and conservative strategy, and he made a very committed and assertive swing. The ball flew as straight as an arrow and came to rest precisely where he had intended.

I had about 250 metres to the hole, so I planned to hit my second shot a distance that would leave around 75 metres. It was slightly downwind and slightly downhill, so 6 iron was good for me. Visually there were a few potential distractions, but I picked an area of dark green grass on the fairway, as though the ancient sage was illuminating the perfect layup position. I chose a conservative target for this layup but committed to an aggressive swing. I visualised the shot, had a practice swing to swing to feel it, and did my standard shirt tug as a trigger for commitment.

CONFIDENCE

As I walked into the hit zone, I felt as though I had stepped out of myself and just observed without any judgement. My mind was quiet, hands and arms soft, legs strong and balanced. A last glance at my target area, a glance that was a soft gaze not a tense stare, eyes back at the ball and without hesitation I made a strong swing, catching the ball right out of the middle of the club. No matter how many thousands of flush shots you have hit, it's still a great feeling that brings great joy and satisfaction, probably similar to that of a winemaker.

The satisfaction a winemaker gets from drinking a successful vintage would be a combination of relief and joy. Relief that they would be financially rewarded for the money invested and effort expended, and that the hard work resulted in a wine that is a joy to drink. Golf is similar as it's an investment in time and often money to hit some good shots, but it's often a huge investment in time and money to hit great shots consistently. I personally have invested decades of time and scraped the bottom of my financial barrel for years on end to get to a point where I consistently hit high-quality shots.

My shot finished precisely where I intended it to. We strolled to our balls, admiring and discussing a newly built house on the perimeter of the golf course. Talk about investment. This house was uniquely built, with bricks that in some places, were only inches in size. The brickwork must have taken months to do. It's easy to overlook the skill and hard work required to achieve certain goals in life. I could only imagine the bricklayers' satisfaction on completion, and the lifelong joy it would bring the homeowners.

Steve had 96 metres, a bit of an in-between distance for him. Too far for his sand wedge so he would have to take a bit off his gap wedge. The pin was a long way back, which was better for Steve as he could grip down on his wedge, which would take some length off the shot and knock the flight down. This would allow him to hit it short of the hole and be released with the wind behind him. I asked Steve what he thought. He said he would hit a mid-flighted shot that would match the fact that he was gripping down on the club, hitting a less than three-quarters shot. I suggested landing it about 86 metres would be good; it would take a bounce, release up and over a small rise in the green, and be on the back level.

He made a nice practice swing, just clipping a few strands of grass. He approached with a softer look to his arms and shoulders than he had in previous holes. He settled over the ball with a soft waggle, made a compact backswing and a great pivot to a short follow-through. It was a crisp strike and looked good in flight. Steve was quiet this time. The ball landed, skipped, and released. This green is very exposed to the wind and with the sun shining, it released more than expected and stopped about 15 feet past the hole. We both thought it would finish closer.

I had 76 metres to the hole and a small tier to negotiate. The top tier feeds downhill to the back of the green, which is an uncommon design. Usually, I like to hit lower shots to back pins, but the tier added greater complexity. I opted to fly it all the way over the small rise to ensure it wouldn't spin back, banking on the ball stopping quickly. I decided on a high lob wedge to fly close to the pin. Given it was an island-like green, I didn't want to aim at the pin, hit it and ricochet into trouble. So, I aimed a metre left of the hole as it was an easier putt from that side.

I came into the shot fully committed, aimed my club then my feet, shuffled a little, looked at the target, breathed deep and easy, my eyes came back to the ball, and I made a nice smooth balanced swing. It felt a touch strong off the club, bounced a metre by the hole, and settled the same distance away as Steve's, just a little more left of the pin.

Steve putted first. His putt had about a foot of left to right break and like all breaking putts, speed determines line, so he needed to be committed to his speed. He took a little bit longer than usual trying to determine his ideal line. He had a couple of practice strokes, looked intently at his line then hit his putt. It appeared to be on a good line but looked as though it needed to roll out. Steve started walking after it as though it was either going in or was going to be short. But unfortunately, it was the latter; he left it about three inches short on a good line.

This can be the result when we get line bound. Golfers can hyper-focus on the line and have too much conscious thought, which then limits the subconscious ability to work to its fullest potential to get the results we want. Sure, you want to choose the right line, but it doesn't necessarily have to be millimetre perfect. A golf hole is 4.25 inches in diameter, allowing for a small margin for error.

Steve's putt had no influence on me. Sure, I'll sometimes watch the speed of someone's ball rolling out, but I certainly didn't need any extra help on this 15-foot slightly left to right putt. It was a straightforward putt and there were no benefits to overcomplicating it. Simplicity over complication every time. I stood over the putt – my newly gripped Lajosi putter felt good in my hands. It's important that your putter is correctly fitted, but it's also very important that you like the look and the feel of your putter, and I certainly liked everything about my putter. With confidence and belief, I hit a great putt out of the sweet spot. I struck the putt, my head still until it had rolled a couple of feet. As I looked up, it was tracking nicely, and I waited for it to move slightly right. It just held its line left to run a foot by the hole. I was satisfied. I did all I could do. I committed to the putt, had no doubts, and made a good stroke but it simply didn't go in. I tapped in my par putt, gave Steve an "I-know-how-you-feel" smile after we both had great chances. We strolled off the green together, taking in the beautiful surrounds of the island green and waterfront homes.

Sage Advice on Confidence

- A truly confident person is one who is always true to their word.
- If you hole 300 consecutive 4-foot putts every day, you will have confidence. Confidence requires work.
- Confidence outsourced is not true confidence.

Confidence

The root word of confidence is "confide", which comes from the Latin word *confidere,* meaning "to trust". Trust is a fundamental requirement for having confidence. Trust is often built over time through consistent and reliable behaviour; it provides the foundations and stability to build confidence. Trust brings an assurance of competence and reliability.

The root word "confide" seems ironic given we confide in ourselves more than anyone else. Confiding in ourselves is not always a positive experience. The truth is we lie to ourselves more than we lie to anyone else. Think of all the times you have said to yourself you would do something, and you haven't done it – go for a walk, send someone an email, catch up with a friend next week – and you didn't do it. You let yourself (and others down), you betrayed your own trust.

To maximise your potential confidence, you need to start by being honest with yourself. Be impeccable with your word. Speak only that which you will do. No excuses. An excuse is a lie that you, or whoever excuses you, is letting you get away with. Every word is a seed, every deed or action is a seed. They need to be seeds of truth that will be congruent with building trust in yourself and producing future confidence.

In any pursuit, we should be seeking mastery. Mastery requires work – quality, mindful practice and refinement of your skill. If you look at an iceberg or a tree, their solid foundations are as deep or bigger than what you see above the ground. If you think about a tree, it establishes a root system to support it before it breaks through. Golfers need to establish strong technical fundamentals to build trust and confidence. But most golfers are deceived by the superior preference of technical work over mindset work. For a swing to hold up under pressure, you need to have a great mindset.

There is not enough importance placed on the mindset by the average golfer. Even top professionals can take too long before they realise the importance of upgrading their mindset in order to gain true confidence and start performing at their peak level.

Given that confidence is an abstract phenomenon and not directly measurable like physical capacities, it is expressed subjectively through behaviour, attitude, and self-expression. Confidence is a state of mind; therefore, it requires state management. Have awareness of your physiology, your breathing, and your muscle tension. Be intentional about your language – the words you speak to maintain a confident state. From the overflow of trust comes permission to pursue your desired outcome. The fuel to maintain confidence is faith – faith being the belief in an outcome you desire.

Sage Questions on Confidence

1. Are there areas in your life or golf where your confidence suffers due to a lack of self-trust?

   _____
   _____
   _____
   _____

2. What processes do you use to maintain a high level of confidence when playing golf?

   _____
   _____
   _____
   _____

3. What do you consider to be the primary source of your confidence?

_____
_____
_____
_____

A Model of Confidence: Tiger Woods

When it comes to confidence, Tiger Woods is a player who has openly expressed his confidence. In an interview before his first-ever professional event, Tiger said to the two-time US Open winner and commentator Curtis Strange, "I'll be winning out there soon." Curtis scoffed and said, "You'll learn," but it was Curtis who learned when Tiger won twice in his rookie year.

But the most dominant display of confidence was Tiger's 2000 US Open win at Pebble Beach. Tiger's 15-stroke victory is the biggest winning margin in US Open history and major golf history. It showcased his self-belief and total trust in his game as he aggressively attacked in each round. Tiger Woods's confidence is the result of a combination of training from a young age, early successes, mental toughness, consistent performance, resilience in the face of adversity and a strong support system. These factors together have contributed to his extraordinary self-belief and confidence throughout his career.

Intention and trust are foundational to confidence. Tiger's success and ability to perform under pressure stem from his deep trust in his abilities and his clear intentions for every shot and round. His confidence wasn't just an abstract feeling; it was built on years of preparation, a solid mental game, and an unwavering belief in his goals.

CHAPTER 17
SELF-BELIEF

"Self-belief is the key that unlocks your great destiny and a fulfilling life, paving the way for limitless possibilities."

Hole 17

The seventeenth hole was a 203 metre challenging par 3. The tee was a little forward, and the pin was towards the front of the green. We had 185 metres to the hole with a slight right-to-left wind, which was helpful on this hole. The left side of the hole was well bunkered, with three bunkers spanning about 50 metres from short left to back left of the green. A spine ran the whole length of the green dividing into left and right as you looked from the tee, albeit on a slight angle of left to right. The pin position was very tight, front left, and brought all the bunkers into play.

I took a 5 iron and aimed at the spine of the green – I anticipated my shot to move a little right to left on the wind and release towards the hole. It was a shot I felt comfortable with. I had a practice swing, felt the shot and walked in confidently with that feel. I aimed my club, set my body to that alignment, shuffling my body with constant little movements. I took my last look at the target, my eyes went back to the ball, and I fired. It came out sweet, right out of the middle of the clubface. The ball was tracking at the spine but not moving as I had anticipated. Sometimes you can just rocket one that the wind doesn't affect.

It landed on the right side of the spine and finished just past pin high, a couple of inches off the right edge of the green. It felt good and I quickly accepted the outcome.

Steve decided on a 4 iron. He, too, was intending on hitting a shot at the green's spine, letting the wind drift it back. He went through his routine. I half watched him, and half looked at the lake and the waterfront homes to our left.

I've always found water to be very peaceful. I have always gone to the beach at times when I needed to find some peace and understanding – a place I have gone to seek God for guidance and answers. I remember once going to the beach in a bit of a huff, demanding I see something tangible from God to prove His existence. I ended up sitting in a blissful state that provided evidence to me that God existed, rather than the something tangible that I was hoping for.

I came back to full focus as Steve had settled over the ball. He took his customary second look and made a swing. It came out a little low on the clubface and also stayed out to the right side. It finished short and right of the hole, about two feet off the green. The right side of the green was a bowl shape. We both had to putt down the right side of the green, then up the hill of the spine, then down the hill to the hole – with multiple breaks.

Although Steve was a couple of feet off the green, he opted to putt. The grass off the green was down grain. Melbourne courses, unlike Queensland, don't have a lot of grain, but this course had its patches. Steve's first half of the putt moved a little left to right, but then once over the spine, it had a little right to left back toward the hole. But as is the case with all breaking putts, speed was the key. He had a couple of nice practice strokes to match the putt he was about to hit. He came into his putt, ran his eyes up the line twice, then made his stroke. The ball made its way down into the bowl, moving left to right up the spine slope, but it was moving quite slowly. After a cry of "get up" from Steve, the ball slowly made its way down the other side of the spine and continued to trickle down. But continue it did; it looked like it was never going to reach the hole, but the

SELF-BELIEF

dried-out green of the afternoon allowed some extra run out. It finished a foot short and left of the hole. Steve sighed, "Wow, I thought I'd left that way short; it just kept going." He tapped his par putt in, albeit after slightly more deliberation than over a normal one-foot putt.

I took in what I saw. My putt was down into the bowl, then up and down the spine, but I had a right-to-left putt all the way. So, after seeing Steve's, I just needed to get my ball to reach the top of the spine with very little speed and let it feed down to the hole. But I was very mindful that I wanted to get over the spine and not have it roll back to me. I was also just off the green, so I missed the benefit of being able to mark and clean my ball; therefore, my putting routine was a little different. I had walked around from my ball around the hole and back to my ball in a 360-degree circle, having a good look, but, more importantly, a good feel in my feet for the putt.

I remember playing with a friend when I was a teenager and we were on the 18th hole at Werribee Park Golf Club, a beautiful golf course in Melbourne's west. It's next to Werribee Park Mansion and Zoo; the Werribee River runs alongside several holes of the golf course with great views from the clubhouse. I recall him saying, "Why do you walk around your putts, sometimes with your eyes closed for a bit?". I replied, "I'm just trying to feel the putt in my feet." He looked at me as though I was mad. I was a late bloomer, both growing and in improving my golf, but I look back and recall picking up some of the finer points of golf by instinct.

I made a couple of practice strokes and looked up the line of the putt ahead. My mind was quiet. I just let myself feel the line, no conscious instructions. I walked into the ball, got my eye line set, then my putter, then my stance. I looked up the line, then once my eyes returned to the ball, I simply reacted to the picture I had just seen with my last look up the line. Down into the bowl it went, up the spine with a bit more speed than Steve's putt, then it started breaking left towards the cup. It just had a little too much speed to take the break and finished three feet past the cup. It wasn't misjudged by much; it was a pretty tricky putt. I grabbed my towel and marked and cleaned my ball. For the first time, I actually felt a little nervous. We were both playing well and a three foot putt is to be respected. The putt was just a fraction left to right; a good speed started on the left edge would be perfect. I have recently spent more time practicing my 3, 5 and 8 foot putts than I ever have, so I was very confident. I committed to my routine, walked into the putt, and made a silky-smooth stroke. The putt came sweetly out of the middle, and I waited until it was dropping in the hole before I raised my eyes. It's very important to maintain a steady head over your putts. With a par on one of the more challenging holes ticked off, it was off to the 18th.

Sage Advice on Self-Belief

- Self-belief is the embodiment of recognising and trusting in our greatest traits, empowering us to achieve excellence.
- Self-belief is a display of knowing your true identity and having great trust in it.
- Self-belief shatters the chains that hold us back, enabling us to overcome obstacles and achieve our desired outcomes.

Self-Belief

Self-belief is crucial in achieving your best in golf and in life. This belief is further enhanced with a greater awareness of your true identity, as opposed to your "lie-dentity", which is the false identity that others impose on you throughout your life. This imposed identity is not your true self, but rather a collection of other's expectations and perceptions that you have come to believe. Discovering your true identity is a highly intentional and often lengthy personal journey towards knowing the truth. If you are serious about pursuing your best golf, you will inevitably be led to find your identity and build your self-belief to an unshakable point.

SELF-BELIEF

Self-belief instils an internal dialogue that is both positive and encouraging. It uses aspects such as resilience to guide you through challenging times, helping you emerge wiser and stronger from each experience. Key aspects of self-belief include knowing your identity, having a healthy opinion of yourself, and significantly, knowing your purpose and your why. Understanding who you truly are, separate from the "lie-dentity" imposed by others, is fundamental. Your real true identity is the foundation upon which self-belief is built.

Self-belief is not something that appears out of thin air; it is cultivated through a combination of trust, intention, and faith. Trust in your abilities, developed through consistent practice and self-honesty, is foundational. Being intentional in your actions ensures that you are not swayed by distractions or self-doubt. Most importantly, having faith in yourself and in your Creator provides the ultimate assurance that you are on the right path, that your efforts are aligned with a greater purpose.

This faith is not just about believing in your potential but also about understanding that you are part of a greater plan, one that requires you to fulfil your purpose with confidence and conviction. This faith in your Creator, rather than the created, roots your self-belief in something far deeper and more resilient than mere self-assurance. It gives you the strength to persevere through challenges and the humility to continue learning and growing.

On the journey to becoming better at golf, you will encounter moments when you play well above your current level. During these times, self-belief is essential to understand and encourage yourself, recognising that this is part of the process of playing your best. Often, golfers feel uncomfortable when they are performing better than their handicap or previous best score. This discomfort stems from their "lie-dentity" and the challenge to their self-belief about their true potential.

Many people do not realise how good they really are. While some may vocalise an overinflated opinion of themselves, this is usually a mechanism to hide their insecurities. More often, people's limited view of themselves and their self-belief holds them back from playing their best golf and living their best life. Self-belief can be strengthened by working through the chapters of this book, which reveal the elements required to develop true self-belief.

You will not have self-belief in your golf game if you don't have it in life – they are inseparable. If you lack the courage or desire to find the best in yourself and live your best life, your golf will never reach its true potential. People who have self-belief live fearlessly. They strive to be their best in all aspects of their lives: their health and fitness, relationships, careers, mindsets, finances, and faith. They are holistic individuals living fulfilling lives.

When you have all the aspects to have self-belief, you become highly resourceful in pursuing your best golf. You seek the best advice on mindset, on swing technique, and fitness. You are mindful and diligent in your practice, enjoying the process of golf mastery. You are resilient when challenged and humble in victory. Self-belief is fundamental to achieving excellence in golf and life. It is intertwined with a deep awareness of your identity, free from the distortions of your "lie-dentity". Knowing your purpose and understanding your why provide additional strength and clarity on this journey. As you work through the different chapters in this book, some may resonate more than others. You will uncover the keys to developing unshakable self-belief, empowering you to live fearlessly and play your best golf. Embrace the journey, for in doing so, you will unlock your true potential and live a life of fulfilment and purpose.

Sage Questions on Self-Belief

1. Reflect on a time when you performed at your best in golf. What internal dialogue and beliefs about yourself were present during that performance, and how can you cultivate those same thoughts and beliefs consistently?

   _____
   _____
   _____
   _____

SELF-BELIEF

2. Consider the concept of your "lie-dentity". In what ways have external expectations and perceptions influenced your view of yourself and your potential in golf and life? How can you begin to cast off these false identities to uncover your true self?

_____
_____
_____
_____

3. Self-belief is vital to living a life of fulfilment. How can you align your beliefs and purposes to the fulfilment of your best life?

_____
_____
_____
_____

Models of Self-Belief: Ben Hogan, Jack Nicklaus and Scottie Scheffler

Time and again, the greats of the game have demonstrated that a fulfilling golf career and life rests on key fundamentals, with self-belief being chief among them. Ben Hogan, Jack Nicklaus and Scottie Scheffler are three such men who stand tall in this regard.

Nicklaus remains the greatest major winner of all time, a record that still holds firm. Many believe Hogan could have challenged that mark if not for his military service and a near-fatal car accident. Both Hogan and Nicklaus distinguished themselves not just by their talent, but by unwavering belief in the games that got them to the top. They trusted their swings, their processes, and themselves. Rather than chase constant change, they refined and reinforced what they already knew worked.

Scottie Scheffler offers a modern and powerful example of this kind of belief, one that was forged through adversity. The morning of his first major championship victory at the U.S. Masters wasn't just a low – it was a rite of passage. He came face-to-face with doubt and chose to overcome it with faith and belief.

Hogan, Nicklaus, and Scheffler all share something deeper than skill or trophies: they are men of faith. Belief in God became a solid foundation for belief in themselves. For each of them, self-belief wasn't self-manufactured, it was deeply rooted in something greater, giving them the strength to hold firm when it mattered most.

CHAPTER 18
BE-DO-HAVE

"As a man thinketh, so shall he be. As a man be, so shall he do and have."

Hole 18

The eighteenth hole was a 403 metre par 4. A picturesque hole with the resort lake all down the left side and an island green, with water about 40 metres short as well as left and behind the green, which was guarded by a big greenside bunker to the right. The clubhouse was down the right side of the hole. We had the good fortune of the hole playing downwind, which was a great advantage. Steve said he felt a little nervous as he'd never broken par, let alone 70. I smiled and said "It was bound to happen someday and today was as good a day as any." I pointed out that the nervous feeling could also be excitement as they present symptomatically very similarly. I think too often people have labelled those stomach butterflies as nerves, whereas excitement had also been present.

I said, "Imagine those early days of dating Sam (Steve's wife). I bet you had a feeling like this." He smiled in response.

I said, "So if you must label it, just say, "Chris, I'm pretty bloody excited."

He smiled and said, "Chris, I'm pretty bloody excited!"

I said, "Good, that's why we practice to where it's pretty bloody exciting." We both smiled as we looked down the fairway. I added, "Well, I'm not sure if the ancient sage meant for all this, but a downwind finish is perfect. I'm going at the cart path in the distance with a little draw, it will bounce off the right-to-left sloping fairway and be in the mayor's office."

I said to Steve, "Mate, we are both driving it great, let's just go through our routines, have faith, which is just believing in the outcome we desire, be the best version of ourselves, and enjoy hitting a good shot."

It's a funny game, golf. You always have so much think time in a round of golf, it can take you on a ride of emotions if you let it. I stood on the tee, thinking of my dad who has passed, and the conversation we would have had after this round.

But I quickly caught my thoughts – target, shape, landing spot. I knew what that meant and I focused on the here and now. I pictured the shot starting at the distant cart path, landing on the right side of the fairway and running into the middle. I took a practice swing to feel the shot, then two steadying breaths behind the ball – hands, arms, shoulders soft. I was the best me right then. I walked into the shot, touched the club down behind the ball, aligned my feet, shuffled my body and got comfortable and ready. I looked at the cart path, then back to the ball, and swung. I felt a little extra pivot speed through the shot and it came out flush. It started right at the cart path, drifted a little left with a draw, and took a nice firm bounce forward into the middle of the fairway.

"Nice shot," said Steve. I thanked him and said, "Yep, that was a nice one to finish on. Just routine and trust, right?"

"Yep, just routine and trust," he said. I replied, "Just be that great you that you have been today, smooth that draw down with mine."

He made a smooth practice swing and walked into the shot, two looks, and made a good swing. It came out high and long. A beaming smile came over his face as he watched it land and release. "Wow, I think that was nearly my best for the day," he said.

I responded with, "That is another benefit of those excitement butterflies; you get a little adrenaline with them, which helps get a few extra metres off the tee."

As we strolled down the fairway, we discussed our plans for the upcoming weekend. Steve had his son's equestrian event, and I had a mindset speaking engagement on Saturday afternoon, followed by dinner with my girls. They love Japanese food, so we usually go out for Japanese after I have any weekend speaking engagements. We approached our balls; Steve was about 15 metres behind my ball. He had 136 metres to a fairly back pin position, just left of centre. The green was slightly elevated from where we were. Steve took an 8 iron. He said to himself, "Righto, at that big window of the grey house in the background. If I imagine hitting my ball through that, it will be perfect."

"Let's see it," I said. "Be who you need to be to hit this great shot."

He made a smooth practice swing. He walked into the ball, focusing on a spot just in front of it. He took his alignment to the big window of the grey house and made a great swing that made a few pieces of grass fly up when he made contact, just as his practice swing had. We both followed it in flight. It landed right centre of the green with a hint of a draw, took two bounces, and rolled to about 30 feet right of the hole. "Good play," I said, "fairly straight uphill putt from there."

I had 121 metres – just a wedge for me. The moment wasn't lost on me. I actually thought back to my approach into the 18th in Vanuatu all those years ago and the lesson of allowing for your miss. I aimed at the middle of the green, about 15 feet right of the hole. I felt excited and confident about the shot. I certainly didn't have the anxiety I had when in Vanuatu. I clipped the grass in my practice swing, focused on keeping a soft consistent tension in my hands, arms, and shoulders. I stood behind the ball, took a couple of deep, slow steadying breaths, walked in calmly, committed to the shot, aimed at the centre of the green, and hit it beautifully crisp. I played the ball about an inch further forward in my stance to give it a little extra height downwind. It took one good bounce, then a small bounce, and stopped almost exactly where I aimed it, 15 feet right of the hole. "Nice shot," said Steve, knowing I had deliberately aimed at the smart side.

The walk to the green was very surreal; it was like having a prayer for the perfect day of golf answered. To play with a long-time best friend, to have perfect spring weather, to have the best rounds of our lives, to feel like we had transformed into being the best version of ourselves – it was an incredible feeling.

As we walked onto the green, we discussed what the putts looked like. Steve's had a touch of left to right as it was just short of pin high, while mine had the smallest amount of right-to-left break, being pretty much pin high. We both marked and cleaned our balls, strolled up and around the hole, and back to our respective putts. I stood to the side as Steve sized up his putt. "All right, great speed," he said out loud, then settled into his routine of a few practice strokes. He took a couple of breaths, which he rarely does. He really steadied himself, and when he approached the ball, he looked confident. He settled into the putt, took his second look and sent the putt on its way. It looked good off the putter, was tracking nicely but just stayed a few inches left. He let out a little exclamation, with as much relief as disappointment in not making a final birdie. Still, he happily tapped in for a 69, his best-ever, and first sub-par round. He took the ball out of the hole, gave a fist pump, and said, "Yes, yes, yes." A combination of elation and satisfaction. In that moment, all the hard work and frustration that almost 40 years of golf had brought him was worth it. He said, "Righto, roll yours in."

I was kneeling behind my ball, looking at the line. I didn't look at him; my focus was on this putt. I acknowledged him with a "Yes," but my focus never deviated. I placed my ball down and removed my sentimental penny. *You got it*, I whispered to myself. *Just roll it on the line, your speed will be perfect*. A couple of deep breaths, and I strolled in, really confident. My eyes, putter and body were aligned. A last look down the line and I made a smooth stroke. As soon as I struck the putt, I knew it was good.

There was a three-ball putting drill I had done over the years. The first ball you putted looking at the hole, the second putt was struck with your eyes closed and you said where it finished before you looked up, and the third ball you putted as normal. Once you did the drill enough, you could get really precise as to where the putt had finished or call it in before it went in.

When I struck this putt, it felt like it was going in. I followed it intensely, a foot from the hole, and started raising my putter triumphantly. I started walking towards the hole knowing it was going in, and indeed it did. I gave a fist pump and a "Yes!" of my own. Steve walked towards me, and we gave each other a fist pump. I picked my ball out of the hole, gave Steve a hug, and said, "Wow, what a day." He picked the pin up and placed it back in the hole.

"Wow, can you believe this day?" he said. We stood on the green, looked around, both took a breath. Steve said, "Wow, that was epic." I agreed, "What a special day."

We walked to our cars. I suggested we get a mineral water and have another roll on the Trigger Point balls to release any tight spots. I like to do this a little before and after golf. Steve agreed and said he'd grab the drinks if I grabbed the balls. I agreed, and we made our way back to the clubhouse.

He said, "Man, you could write a book about that round and this day."

I said, "Yes, I think I probably could."

Sage Advice on Be-Do-Have

- An empowering coaching tool, used since the beginning of time.
- The winner's way of obtaining your desired outcomes.
- The quickest way to transform into the best version of yourself.

Be-Do-Have

The be-do-have coaching model is a very popular tool among life and mindset coaching professionals. Its origins go back to the first words God spoke to Adam, "Be fruitful"– the be. "Multiply and replenish the earth" – the do. "And have dominion over the birds of the air, the fish of the sea, and every living creature on the earth" – the have. To be fruitful is to produce on the outside what is on the inside. You have great desires that you have not yet fulfilled. You have seeds inside of you that have not yet been fruitful. You have got your best score inside of you that is ready to bear fruit, ready to be fruitful. Instead of asking what you have to do to get the results you want, ask a better question: Who do you need to be? What type of person do you need to be to get the results and outcomes you desire?

The overflow of upgrading who you are being will result in an upgrade in what you do and what you have. In order for you to become a better version of yourself, you need to surrender to the old you. Just as a seed had to stop being a seed in order to become a tree and a caterpillar had to stop being a caterpillar to become a butterfly, you must be prepared to leave disempowering thoughts and behaviours behind to become a better you.

Often, this type of transformation tool requires you to begin with the end in mind. Picture the outcomes you desire. Picture who you need to be to get what you desire, and then embody who you need to be to get those outcomes. Model yourself on the people who have what you desire. How do they speak, what clothes do they wear, how do they carry themselves? But maintain your authenticity; just utilise certain aspects of their being that will benefit you. You are the only you out of the billions of people who live or have lived on this earth. Just as no one can be a better version of you, you cannot be a better version of someone else. So don't lose your essence in the process of modelling someone else. Stay true to your values and your essence.

Sage Questions on Be-Do-Have

1. Are you clear about who you need to be in order to live a fruitful life? Can you describe the mindset and characteristics of your best self?
   _____
   _____
   _____
   _____

2. Are you clear about the type of person you need to be to play your best golf? What are some of the key traits that define this version of yourself?
   _____
   _____
   _____
   _____

3. What obstacles or kryptonite hinder your ability to consistently be the golfer you aspire to be? How can you address these challenges?
   _____
   _____
   _____
   _____

Be-Do-Have: Your Story

Each chapter in this book has used examples of a champion golfer to help you remember the application of the coaching tool and the power in the coaching tool. It is my hope that the most inspiring Be-Do-Have story is going yours in the coming years. That through the seeds inside of you, you will envision who you need to be to achieve your golf and life desires. From the vision and clarity of who you need to be and with the wisdom of books like this, you will know what to do. And the being and the doing will enable you to have and live out your best golf and your best life. There are benefits in studying and modelling the greats of golf and life, but your mission is the same as what God said to the first man in Adam, "Be fruitful, multiply, and replenish the earth, and have dominion."

Be the best you, use your courage, and take action to live a fulfilling life. Now it's time for you to start writing your story.

_____
_____
_____
_____
_____
_____
_____
_____
_____
_____
_____

Final Thoughts: Embrace the Journey

As you close this book, take a moment to reflect on the journey you've embarked upon. The lessons, stories, and wisdom contained within these pages are not just for reading – they are a call to action. They have invited you to step into a new level of being, doing, and having, where your greatest potential is realised, and your dreams are within reach.

Golf, like life, is a journey filled with challenges, triumphs, and moments of profound learning. It's a game that mirrors the ups and downs we all experience. But as you've learned, the key to mastering both is in mastering yourself.

Every chapter offers you the tools to build a foundation of self-belief, intention, trust, resilience, and mastery. These are not just abstract concepts; they are the bedrock of a fulfilled life, on and off the course.

Be intentional. Be resilient. Be the person you aspire to be. With every swing, every decision, every challenge, let your actions be guided by the principles you've discovered in this book. Remember, the greatest victories are won within. Your mindset, your beliefs, your trust in yourself, and in your Creator – these are the true determinants of your success.

The seeds of greatness are already within you. Just as each champion has shown, your best golf and your best life are waiting to be unlocked by those who choose to be today.

So, step forward with confidence. Embrace the journey with faith, intention, and the knowledge that you are capable of far more than you've ever imagined. The seeds of greatness are already within you. Now it's time to nurture them, to be fruitful, and to live the extraordinary life you were created to live.

Here's to you playing your best golf and living a life of great fulfilment.

ABOUT THE AUTHOR

Chris Hynes

An Australian PGA member since 2000, Chris Hynes' journey in golf has been anything but conventional. After initially struggling to fulfill his potential as a player, Chris pursued a successful career as a personal trainer for over 20 years. During this time, he also worked as a professional blackjack player, sharpening his focus, discipline and strategic thinking.

During a break from professional golf, Chris ventured into competitive boxing, an experience that profoundly impacted his life. It strengthened him physically, mentally and spiritually, instilling a robust work ethic, resilience and a deep belief in his own strengths. The discipline and perseverance he developed in the ring became invaluable tools that he carried back into his journey as a golfer, coach, and mindset mentor.

His own journey of personal development and transformation rekindled his passion for the game, especially after completing his studies as a mindset coach. Today, Chris is dedicated to empowering golfers to unlock their true potential, combining his expertise in fitness, strategy and mindset.

As the author of *Beyond the Fairways to Fulfilment*, Chris is intentional about sharing his model for success with golfers, athletes, leaders and anyone seeking to elevate their life and performance. He facilitates world-class mindset programs and delivers impactful keynote speeches, grounded in the principles and concepts of his book.

When Chris isn't coaching or writing, he enjoys spending time with his daughters and continuing to refine his craft, both on and off the course.

You can contact Chris via:
Email: **chrishynescoaching@outlook.com**
Instagram: **chris_hynes_coaching**

www.ingramcontent.com/pod-product-compliance
Lightning Source LLC
LaVergne TN
LVHW090116080426
835507LV00040B/913